C000131803

When angels sat down

105 Devotional readings

Gordon Kell

Scripture Truth Publications

Reader reviews for
Footsteps in the Snow

"Thank you so much for ... your daily posts.
What a help and encouragement they have been
throughout this challenging year!"

"How often the message every morning has been
so appropriate to the difficulties which we have
been experiencing."

"Thank you for your encouraging and sometimes
challenging words... So often, they were just what
we needed to hear that day!"

"The ministry the Lord has given you during this
past year has drawn us closer to the Lord and to
one another."

When Angels sat Down

105 Devotional readings

FIRST EDITION

FIRST PRINTING March 2022

ISBN: 978-0-9511515-8-7 (paperback)

Copyright © 2021 Gordon Kell and Scripture Truth Publications in this edition

A publication of Scripture Truth

Published by Scripture Truth Publications
31-33 Glover Street, Crewe, Cheshire, CW1 3LD

Scripture Truth is an imprint of Central Bible Hammond Trust, a charitable trust

Cover design by Gwyneth Duff
Typesetting by Helen Jones

This book is dedicated to Dr. John Rice whose friendship, fellowship and wholehearted commitment to the work of STP I have so much appreciated.

Contents

Joseph

Aquila and Priscilla

Nehemiah

Barnabas

The Armour of God

Faith

List of Abbreviations

AV – Authorised (King James) Version

ch. – chapter

ESV – English Standard Version

LXX – Septuagint (the ancient Greek translation of the Old Testament)

NIV – New International Version

NLT – New living Translation

v. – verse

vv. – verses

Preface

I wrote *Footsteps in the Snow* as a series of devotional readings during the first three months or so of the COVID-19 restrictions in the UK. For some time I had had it in mind to write a book of short reflections on verses from the Bible. COVID isolation provided the opportunity to do this. My aim was to stimulate fellowship with Christ through the daily reading of the Bible. The Lord makes it clear in John 15 that "without Me you can do nothing" (v. 5). The power of the Christian life comes from abiding in Him (v. 4). So, I wanted to provide short Christ-centred articles that would focus our hearts and minds on the Person of Christ and all the spiritual resources we find in Him. *When Angels Sat Down* continues this theme.

The content of *When Angels Sat Down* and its predecessor *Footsteps in the Snow* emerged from the author's own early morning daily reflections, which were shared with Christians in the UK and overseas. The book offers a mixture of stand-alone articles and several mini-series based on biblical themes and characters. They are set out, with one or two exceptions, in their written order.

It is essential to cultivate a daily spiritual fellowship with Christ. The Bible is central to this experience. Like Mary and Martha in Luke 10 we discover that one thing is necessary. This is to sit in the presence of the Saviour. By doing so, we are empowered to express the life, the mind, the Person and the strength of Jesus Christ. I hope this book will stimulate our communion with Christ.

Acknowledgements

The manuscript of *When Angels Sat Down* was edited by John Broadley. Helen Jones prepared the layout and undertook the final proofreading. Gwyneth Duff has once more designed an excellent cover. I would like to acknowledge John, Helen and Gwyneth's considerable work and to thank them for making this book possible.

Introduction

The theme of *When Angels Sat Down* is taken from Day 61 in *Footsteps in the Snow*. That article focuses on two passages. The first is in Matthew 28: "An angel of the Lord descended from heaven, and came and rolled back the stone from the door, and sat on it" (v. 2). The second is in John 20: "And she (Mary) saw two angels in white sitting, one at the head and the other at the feet, where the body of Jesus had lain (v. 12). Angels were present at the birth of Jesus. They ministered to Him after He was confronted by Satan in the wilderness and in the Garden of Gethsemane. Before going to the cross, Christ said He could call on more than twelve legions of angels (Matthew 26:53). But the Lord's work of salvation at Calvary was entirely His own: the angels could only stand in wonder as the Lord of life sacrificed His life for our redemption.

Angels, however, were present to announce His resurrection. And it is at the resurrection we see them doing something they were not created to do. They sat down. Angels are the ministers of God and constantly fulfil holy activities. So to see them sitting down is very interesting. In the simple acts of sitting down on the stone that was rolled away and in the place where Jesus had been lain in the tomb we have vivid reminders of the finished work of Christ and the glory of His resurrection.

This series of books was written to be read day by day or simply opened at any page to find a self-contained reflection on a Bible passage. In is intended that these bite-sized readings would stimulate daily Bible reading and encourage further study. The readings that appear on Sundays have a particular reference to worshipping the Lord in the light of His request that we remember His death (see Luke 22:19-20 and 1 Corinthians 11:23-26). It appears from Acts 20:7 to be a practice the early church adopted. From this place of worship, I believe we enter each new week in discipleship and service. By remembering Christ's love for us, we are inspired to serve Him and each other in love.

I hope that *When Angels Sat Down* will encourage its readers, like the angels, to pause and reflect on the power and majesty of the Person and work of Jesus.

Day 1

Sunday

1 Corinthians 13: The language of love

Though I speak with the tongues of men and of angels, but have not love, I have become as sounding brass or a clanging cymbal

(1 Corinthians 13:1)

---

1 Corinthians 13 describes love in the most profound and beautiful terms. It has been described as a "hymn of love". It is also a parenthesis, because it comes amid Paul's teaching on the spiritual gifts which so occupied the Corinthian Christians. The beauty of its language has a tremendous impression on everyone who reads it. It is regarded as one of the most outstanding pieces of literature in any language. But the chapter is one of the most challenging passages in the Bible. And its teaching should reach into our hearts and souls and transform our lives.

The Bible teaches that God is love. 1 Corinthians 13 expounds the reality of that love. In doing so, it cuts through the unclear and sentimental approach we sometimes have to this vital subject. The chapter begins strikingly and directly. Paul says it doesn't matter how eloquent and beautiful our words are; unless they are spoken in love, they are empty. As with most introductions, we can skip over the words we read without thinking too deeply about them. But as I reread these well-known verses, I had to stop and reflect. We can preach, minister, pray and worship using lovely expressions. But do I always serve the Lord, His people and my neighbours in love? How quickly do words spoken to heaven change to words of criticism, irritation, impatience or anger on earth?

Love is always active and ever serves, but not always audibly. In Luke 7 Jesus describes the worshipping woman as loving much because she was forgiven much (see v. 47). She never spoke a word. Love speaks in simplicity through selflessness and sacrifice. And as the Spirit of God teaches us about the character of love, He wants us to look at the One who perfectly expressed God's heart of love, the Lord Jesus. Today's chapter describes the love we see in Jesus, but it starts by challenging what we say and what we do, and asks, Is it said and done in love?

In Hebrews 4:12 we read, "For the word of God is alive and active. Sharper than any double-edged sword, it penetrates even to dividing soul and spirit, joints and marrow; it judges the thoughts and attitudes of the heart" (NIV). In 1 Corinthians Paul is ministering in love to a large but disorderly church. Paul does not disown the saints at Corinth, nor does he simply judge them. In love, by the Holy Spirit, he exposes the reality of their need and clears the ground so that God can pour His love into their hearts.

Love is a gift. Throughout our lives we need to remember that God is the source of everything we have and are. God is love, and He expressed this by giving: "God so loved that He gave his only begotten son"; "Christ loved the Church and gave Himself for her"; "The Son of God loved me and gave Himself for me." Because "He first loved us", we love. It is in appreciating the love of God for us that His love is manifested through us. We read in Romans 5:5: "The love of God has been poured out in our hearts by the Holy Spirit who was given to us." To pour out such love, the Lord Jesus "poured out His soul unto death" (Isaiah 53:12).

Day 2

Monday

1 Corinthians 13: Acting in love

And though I have the gift of prophecy, and understand all mysteries and all knowledge, and though I have all faith, so that I could remove mountains, but have not love, I am nothing. And though I bestow all my goods to feed the poor, and though I give my body to be burned, but have not love, it profits me nothing.

(1 Corinthians 13:2-3)

In these verses Paul lists the gifts of prophecy, understanding, faith and sacrifice. These are all needed to build up the people of God. Prophecy reveals the mind of God in terms of the past, present and the future. Understanding brings us into an appreciation of all that God is doing. Faith demonstrates our complete trust in God in the ordinary and extraordinary experiences of life. And sacrificial giving benefits others. But Paul surprises us by saying that all these things can be done without love.

Paul had been transformed by the love of Christ. He never ever forgot that Christ loved him even when he had used all his influence, gifts and energy to destroy the Christian Church. It was the love of Christ which compelled Paul to minister in love to the people he once persecuted. This love was the basis of his first epistle to the Corinthians. By the Spirit of God, he highlighted how the love of God was evidently lacking amongst them. In the Old Testament God had to highlight the hypocrisy of the nation of Israel. Their outward behaviour suggested a spiritual life, yet their hearts were far from God. The Lord Jesus condemned the practice of the Pharisees. And, as we are seeing, Paul has to address similar problems in Corinth. The Church has been afflicted in the same way ever since. And love has to expose such failure in order to change it.

In verse 3 the Apostle surprises us by focusing on the sacrificial giving of all material goods for the benefit of those in greatest need, The National Lottery provides a fascinating insight into human nature. Its principle is simple and effective. Funds raised are distributed to different causes. Give people the incentive of enormous prizes, and they will buy tickets, even though the likelihood of winning is extremely remote. Remove the lottery factor, and the giving diminishes. Why do we need to have the possibility of gaining something before we give? What is lacking? He also speaks of the sacrifice of life itself. People can be willing to sacrifice everything in the pursuit of a cause. In our time, we have seen the emergence of suicide bombing. These dreadful actions involve the complete sacrifice of a life to completely destroy the lives of others: giving life to destroy life. The motives for sacrifice are not always marked by purity and can be based on pure hatred. We believe in the Lord Jesus Christ, who sacrificed Himself in love so that we could live in His love.

Paul was asking the Christians at Corinth, and Christians today, about their motives. Do we express the love that redeemed us, or do we tend to act in self-interest, even in spiritual matters? He challenges the basis of our communications, understanding, faith and practice with one incisive question, "Does the love of Christ motivate us?" The Holy Spirit in love exposes our behaviour in order to transform it. Looking into our hearts prepares us to look at the heart of Christ. We should not be afraid, guided by the Spirit of God, to search within to judge our motives. This will lead us to the One who will reassure us of His love for us and teach us to live in its power.

"Yes, I have loved you with an everlasting love;
Therefore with lovingkindness I have drawn you"
(Jeremiah 31:3).

Day 3

Tuesday

1 Corinthians 13: Love suffers long...

Love suffers long and is kind; love does not envy; love does not parade itself, is not puffed up.   *(1 Corinthians 13:4)*

It is touching that Paul first describes love as patient and kind. This also brings into focus Paul's personal experience of the love of Christ. Jesus said to him from heaven, "Why do you persecute me?" The Lord Jesus was simultaneously revealing His love for His Church on earth and His love for the one who was persecuting it. Someone has said, "The proof of love is its capacity to suffer for the object of its affection." Paul later writes, "When the kindness and the love of God our Saviour toward man appeared ..." (Titus 3:4). This was seen in the Person of Christ here in this world. And it is known by every one of us when it dawns in all its brightness and healing power in our hearts.

God's love, displayed in patience and kindness, does not cease. It was there before we knew it, it was there at our salvation, and it never stops being active towards us. In our relationships we discover how difficult it is to bear with people even when we love them dearly. It is also challenging to be consistently kind, especially when our love is rebuffed. Paul is not saying love is easy; he is telling us what it is. Love is often rejected, but real love remains consistent. Patience is characteristic of the way God deals with us. In the words of 2 Peter 3:9: "The Lord is not slack concerning His promise, as some count slackness, but is longsuffering toward us, not willing that any should perish but that all should come to repentance." God is love and Christians are to manifest the love of their Father by showing patience and kindness towards each other and towards everyone.

After beginning to describe what love is, Paul next begins to describe what it is not. He starts by telling us love does not envy. He goes right to the heart of evil. Satan envied God. Satan brought envy into the hearts of our first parents. Envy is about wanting what we do not have, and what we could never have. Envy is about self. Love looks outwards, envy looks inwards. Envy is the force which would seek to rob others and reward me. Love is about blessing others at my expense.

Love does not "parade" itself. The Lord Jesus condemned the Pharisees for taking every opportunity to let others know about their righteousness. They "paraded" what they considered were their good deeds. It is human nature to want others to know what we have done. But love does not need to display itself or seek admiration. It has the humility which Paul brings before our hearts in the Person of the Lord Jesus in Philippians 2:

> Let nothing be done through selfish ambition or conceit, but in lowliness of mind let each esteem others better than himself. Let each of you look out not only for his own interests, but also for the interests of others. Let this mind be in you which was also in Christ Jesus, who, being in the form of God, did not consider it robbery to be equal with God, but made Himself of no reputation, taking the form of a bondservant, and coming in the likeness of men. And being found in appearance as a man, He humbled Himself and became obedient to the point of death, even the death of the cross" (vv. 3-8).

We learn to love from the One who is love.

Day 4

Wednesday

1 Corinthians 13: Love does not...

Love does not behave rudely, does not seek its own, is not provoked, thinks no evil. Love also does not rejoice in iniquity, but rejoices in the truth; bears all things, believes all things, hopes all things, endures all things. (1 Corinthians 13:5-7)

Paul is straightforward in these verses. He was speaking to Christians who were failing to demonstrate the love of Christ. We are all capable of rudeness, wanting our own way, being provoked to anger and retaliation, and finding fault. But these are not excuses. God has given His Holy Spirit who manifests in us love, joy and peace. Rudeness is replaced by longsuffering, kindness, and goodness (Galatians 5:22). Having the mind of Christ removes selfish ambition and conceit. Instead, in lowliness, we esteem others better than ourselves. We don't just look after ourselves, but we care for each other (Philippians 2:3-8). The fruit of the Spirit includes the power to be self-controlled. Instead of being provoked to anger and retaliation, we respond in love to stir up each other to love and good works (Hebrews 10:24).

We live in a world that rejoices in iniquity. It has an unhealthy preoccupation with immoral behaviour and wickedness. This is often presented in the guise of the freedom of the press, but betrays a spirit of delight whenever it can spread across its front pages the failures, downfall and humiliation of celebrity, politician and ordinary citizen alike. King David was overwhelmed with sorrow when he heard his enemy Saul was dead. He said,

"The beauty of Israel is slain on your high places!
How the mighty have fallen" (2 Samuel 1:19).

We should never find pleasure in absorbing news of wickedness, nor in the belittling of the sufferings of others. Love sorrows over sin and always seeks God's salvation for others.

Love rejoices in the truth. The Lord describes Himself as the truth: "I am the way, the truth, and the life'" (John 14:6). In John 17:17 Jesus says, "Sanctify them by Your truth. Your word is truth." We find Christ in the Scriptures. Through them we experience the sanctifying effect of the word of God in our lives. It produces in us the love which bears, believes, hopes and endures all things. Ultimately we discover "all things work together for good to those who love God, to those who are the called according to His purpose" (Romans 8:28).

"Bearing all things" is love demonstrated in our care for others. "Enduring all things" is love shown in our circumstances, however testing: "Looking unto Jesus, the author and finisher of our faith, who for the joy that was set before Him endured the cross" (Hebrews 12:2). Love also believes all things. This is about the present. We should believe and live in the good of all the promises of God. We should also view people and events in the best light and not immediately think evil of other people. Love also hopes all things. This is about the future. Love is nurtured by the word of God and rejoices in doing His will today, trusting the love of Christ will bring blessing. It also has complete confidence in knowing the God who holds the future. His love never fails.

Day 5

1 Corinthians 13: Love never fails

*Love never fails. But whether there are prophecies, they will
fail; whether there are tongues, they will cease; whether there is
knowledge, it will vanish away. For we know in part and we
prophesy in part.* (1 Corinthians 13: 8-9)

The love of God never fails. The reality of this is seen in the
Lord Jesus. We trace it in the incarnation when God entered
His creation. It was displayed in Christ's words of grace and
His power to heal and forgive. And ultimately we see His
profound and unfailing love in His death at Calvary. This was
the place where Jew and Gentile, energised by Satan, rejected
and crucified the Lord of Glory. The time came when man
and Satan were put aside. Darkness fell. And God brought His
judgement against sin upon the Saviour. God "did not spare
his own Son, but gave him up for us all" (Romans 8:32). But
nothing which man, Satan or God's judgement was able to do
could ever extinguish the love that "laboured in His breaking
heart". His love did not fail or end:

> Many waters cannot quench love,
> Nor can the floods drown it" (Song of Solomon 8:7).

Christ's sufferings did not extinguish His love: they manifested
its wonder and power. At Calvary we hear those wondrous
words, "It is finished" (John 19:30) and we listen to the voice
of the Shepherd who had the power to lay down His life for us
in love: "Father, into Your hands I commit My spirit" (Luke
23:46; cf. John 10:18).

We have reminded ourselves over and over again during lockdown of Romans 8:38-39:

> For I am persuaded that neither death nor life, nor angels nor principalities nor powers, nor things present nor things to come, nor height nor depth, nor any other created thing, shall be able to separate us from the love of God which is in Christ Jesus our Lord.

God is love. And because He is eternal, His love cannot fail. This cannot be said of even the greatest of gifts. Prophecies come to an end, having fulfilled their purpose. Tongues will cease; they will not be needed in a coming day. Knowledge will "vanish away", as the Apostle describes in the next few verses. Knowledge and prophesying are never entirely complete. We look forward to the day when we shall come into all the fullness and clarity of the love of God.

We prove in our lives now the love that does not end. We experience within the confines of time and the human condition the wonder of eternal love. Moment by moment that love is active and powerful. God embraces all His people within His love. He is able to hear and respond to all our needs simultaneously. He upholds, in incomprehensible power, not only the observable universe but the unseen spiritual world.

This morning, churches and meeting rooms will re-open across the UK, and the people of God will gather together in them in large and small numbers. They will also meet in their own homes in twos or threes and even in complete isolation. It is His unfailing love that binds us together and makes us one. In that love we will look back to the cross. In faith we will look up to our risen and glorified Saviour and Lord with the hope of His return in our hearts. His love will fill our hearts with worship and the joy of telling the Father of all His glory.

Day 6

Friday

1 Corinthians 13: Faith, Hope, Love

But when that which is perfect has come, then that which is in part will be done away. When I was a child, I spoke as a child, I understood as a child, I thought as a child; but when I became a man, I put away childish things. For now, we see in a mirror, dimly, but then face to face. Now I know in part, but then I shall know just as I also am known. And now abide faith, hope, love, these three; but the greatest of these is love.

(1 Crinthians 13:10-13)

In these verses Paul looks forward to an eternal day of perfection. In that day all the partial knowledge and understanding we have now will be superseded. He illustrates this with his own transition from childhood to maturity. When he became a man, he saw things with a clarity he never had as a child. He contrasts our present condition with our future heavenly position. "For our citizenship is in heaven, from which we also eagerly wait for the Saviour, the Lord Jesus Christ, who will transform our lowly body that it may be conformed to His glorious body, according to the working by which He is able even to subdue all things to Himself" (Philippians 3:20-21).

Paul recognises the limitations of our present circumstances and speaks with absolute certainty of the coming perfect eternal Day of God. Now we are in the dimension of time and the confines of our humanity. Now spiritual gifts are precious assets. They are given by God in Romans 12, empowered by the Holy Spirit in 1 Corinthians 12, and are the fruits of the victorious Christ in Ephesians 4. They are vital for the building up of the people of God, but they will fulfil their purpose and run their course. Knowledge and prophesying, even when ministered in the power of the Spirit, give a partial view of eternal things. This environment of imperfection keeps us humble and exercises our faith, hope and love. Paul, for all his many spiritual gifts, lived his life looking up to Christ in glory and living in the power of the hope he had in Him. Although our vision is imperfect, we are given the assurance that, in the future, we shall know as we are known. No more mysteries, confusion or unanswered questions, but shining, holy, clarity! It is incredible to think that, in a future day, not only will the great questions be answered but also all the tiny aspects of our lives will be unfolded, and the purposes of God fully revealed. We are thankful to God for knowledge and prophecies. But faith, hope and love all look beyond time to God's ultimate purposes fulfilled in Christ.

The three aspects of God's life in us are faith, hope and love. Faith is exercised now. It makes the things of God real to our hearts now and stimulates faithful and holy living. Hope is about the future and will be fulfilled in an instant (see 1 Corinthians 15:51-53). Our hope is in the Lord Jesus and purifies us as He is pure (1 John 3:2-3). Faith will give way to sight, and hope will be fulfilled. Love is eternal. Our destiny is to be embraced by and respond to the love of God eternally: "For I consider that the sufferings of this present time are not worthy to be compared with the glory which shall be revealed in us" (Romans 8:18).

Augustine said, "One loving heart sets another on fire." 1 Corinthians 13 presents the love of Christ to set our hearts on fire to worship, follow and serve the Lord Jesus in faith, hope and love, in fellowship with one another, until the perfect day.

Day 7

Preaching in a barn

Therefore those who were scattered went everywhere preaching the word. *(Acts 8:4)*

An evangelist was cycling between two villages and it was a very warm day. As he cycled along, he saw a large barn in the field alongside the road he was travelling on. For some reason he felt the urge to preach the Gospel in the barn. But then he thought … it was a warm day, he was tired and his mind was playing a trick on him. So he carried on. But as he travelled, the barn stayed in view and the compulsion to preach in it became stronger. At last he got off his bike and walked across the field and into the barn. Like most barns, there was a lot of hay and an absence of people. But to fulfil the urge to preach, he stood in the middle of the building and at the top of his voice shouted, "For God so loved the world that He gave His only begotten Son, that whoever believes in Him should not perish but have everlasting life" (John 3:16). Then he left the barn, got back on his bike and cycled on his way.

Some months later, he was preaching in a local church. He recounted his experience in the barn and told his listeners he couldn't understand why he felt God led him to go there and shout out John 3:16. After the meeting, he discovered why. A young man approached him and shook him warmly by the hand. He explained he had been working near the barn the evangelist had spoken about. On such a warm day, he had taken a nap in the hay. He was woken up by the words of John 3:16. The speaker had disappeared, but as well as waking up from sleep he had woken up spiritually and soon opened his heart to the Lord.

This incident gives us an insight into how, in the ordinariness of a journey, God can do something remarkable and lead us to the precise place He wants us to be. Most times it will not be a compulsion to visit a barn: it will, most probably, be in very commonplace circumstances. We have grown up with formal meetings in which the Gospel is communicated, and God continues to bless this ministry. But it has struck me afresh how the ministry of Christ and of the apostles was so often fulfilled by being actively engaged with people from all walks of life and in all the circumstances of life. The Lord sought and found beggars, and rulers of the synagogue. He was present at the joy of a wedding, and the sorrow of a funeral. He was inside houses, and outside in fields. The Lord Jesus was sensitive to every need. This same grace was evident in the early church and, strikingly, even persecution never restrained the Gospel, but only served to ensure its expansion.

So often we look for a special ministry and can overlook the opportunities everyday life provides. A Christian once said to an evangelist that he wished he could be an evangelist. The evangelist asked him what job he did and the man told him he had a market stall. Then the evangelist asked him how many people visited his stall; he explained he had lots of customers every day. The evangelist said it seemed to him that his friend already had a pulpit: he just needed to use it! This challenges all of us. And perhaps more than ever in the present circumstances, God would lead us to those whose hearts He wants to open to the Saviour: "And they went out and preached everywhere, the Lord working with them and confirming the word through the accompanying signs. Amen" (Mark 16:20).

Day 8

Sunday

This my body ... this is my blood

And He took bread, gave thanks and broke it, and gave it to them, saying, "This is My body which is given for you; do this in remembrance of Me." Likewise He also took the cup after supper, saying, "This cup is the new covenant in My blood, which is shed for you. *(Luke 22:19-20)*

It fills me with wonder how the Lord Jesus conveys to our hearts the depth of His profound love in the simplest of ways. He took two of the most commonplace items of food and drink. He describes the loaf as, "My body given for you" and the cup of wine as, "My blood shed for you".

The early church appears to have quickly established the practice of remembering the Lord at the beginning of the week: "... on the first day of the week, when the disciples came together to break bread" (Acts 20:7). This was the day when Jesus rose from among the dead, a constant reminder of the love that was stronger than death. It makes complete spiritual sense that we start the week responding to the Lord's request to remember Him. I have heard it argued that we should not break bread too frequently lest we take it for granted. We would never say, "Let's not preach the Gospel too often in case people become too familiar with it." So why would we think thus of the love of Christ which is the basis of the Gospel?

But it is right to be reminded that Christ's love should never be taken for granted. The Ephesian church was richly blessed. It was to this church Paul wrote, "And walk in love, as Christ also has loved us and given Himself for us, an offering and a sacrifice to God for a sweet-smelling aroma (Ephesians 5:2). Paul reminds them of Christ's sacrifice to empower them to walk in love. In the same chapter he writes, "Husbands, love your wives, just as Christ also loved the church and gave Himself for her" (Ephesians 5:25). The power to express the love of Christ comes from never forgetting its depth and its cost. Yet, it was to the Ephesian church the Lord says, "Nevertheless I have this against you, that you have left your first love. Remember therefore from where you have fallen; repent and do the first works" (Revelation 2:4-5). In the previous verses the Lord Jesus had commended them for their hard work, patience, practical holiness and faithfulness. But their love for the Lord had diminished and no longer reigned in their hearts as it once did. It is a solemn thing to realise we can be in love with what we do in our particular fellowships, large and small, yet lose our first love for the Lord. In encouraging them to re-ignite this love, it is very striking that the Lord Jesus uses the word "Remember".

When we remember the Lord, the focus is on Him and the wonder of His redeeming love and His immense sacrifice for us. It is a time when we put everything else to one side and simply do what He asked us to do – remember Him. We are to come ready to express our gratitude both in the quietness of our individual hearts and in fellowship with the people of God to praise, sing, read the Scriptures and break the one loaf and drink from the one cup. In that hour, we 'make Him a supper' (see John 12:2). And we discover afresh that He has 'brought us into His banqueting house, and His banner over us is love' (see Song of Solomon 2:4). This is the place where we discover afresh how much we are loved. And it is from this place we go to express His love in our hard work, patience, practical holiness and faithfulness.

Day 9

Monday

Hannah, a wife

But Hannah had no children. *(1 Samuel 1:2)*

Hannah is one of the great women of faith in the Bible. She was the mother of Samuel, one of God's greatest prophets. His ministry began at the darkest hour of Israel's history and led to the dawn of its greatest era under King David and his son Solomon. To understand his spiritual roots we have to look at the life of his remarkable mother. She teaches us lessons from events which took place thousands of years ago and yet are powerfully relevant today. We find her story in 1 Samuel 1. It is the story of one woman's spiritual experience with God. It is a story which affected her life, her marriage, her family and her nation. It is the story of a wife.

Hannah had a lot going for her. She lived in a godly home and she had a good husband, called Elkanah, who loved her. Hannah's story reminds us of some of the important ingredients of successful marriage and family life. First of all, the worship of God was central to the home (v. 3). Elkanah took responsibility for the spiritual and material welfare of his wives and children (vv. 3-5). This balance is critical to Christian marriage.

The Bible clearly teaches us about family life and its responsibilities in passages such as Ephesians 5:22-6:4. And in 1 Timothy 5:8 Paul explains the importance of providing for our families. The roles of the husband and wife are balanced but, as we shall see, the wife has pivotal responsibilities in relation to the spiritual welfare of her husband and her children. The

Christian home is a testimony to God's pattern of life in a world where marriage and the family are under constant threat.

The strength of love which Elkanah had for Hannah is underlined in verse 5. It was an unconditional love. Hannah had no children – in a culture were motherhood was central and children regarded as a sign of blessing. Elkanah's love for his wife did not diminish in spite of this disappointment. Today, there is always the danger of marriage breakdown because husbands and wives do not meet up to each other's expectations. The pattern for the Christian is to conquer the difficulties, which marriages often face, with the kind of love which characterised the marriage of Elkanah and Hannah. Abraham and Sarah in the book of Genesis, and Joseph and Mary in the Gospels, are other outstanding examples of how love and faithfulness conquered the most testing circumstances.

However, the pain of Hannah's childlessness was real. But more than this, we are told twice in verses 5 and 6 that it was the Lord who had prevented her from having children. This is fundamental to the story of Hannah. Why did God deliberately prevent this godly woman from having the children she so much desired?

God sometimes allows us to enter into difficult and painful circumstances so that we can prove our faith in Him, and also for blessing that extends beyond the circumstances in which it is experienced. Faith is tested to prove its reality. A German friend of mine, who was an engineer, once explained to me that bridges are tested well beyond the loads they are expected to bear before being put into service. The testing is not to prove the weakness of the structure but to prove its strength. God allows us to face problems in our lives, not to destroy our faith but to strengthen it and to demonstrate its genuineness. Hannah teaches us about real faith in real circumstances. In doing so, her life is an inspiration to us to have an unfailing trust in God in the conditions He has placed us.

Day 10

Hannah's distress

Therefore she wept. (1 Samuel 1:7)

It is all very well for me to write that there are times when God allows us to enter into difficult circumstances so that we have the opportunity to prove our faith in Him. But what about the genuine pain and distress which we experience? Hannah felt the bitterness of her situation, and the cruelty of Peninnah, Elkanah's other wife (v. 6). (It was never in the will of God that a man should have more than one wife and Christianity re-established this principle; see 1 Timothy 3:2,12; Titus 1:6). One of the hardest of all Christian lessons is to display the features of Christ in painful and unjust circumstances. Yet it is precisely in those situations that the reality of Christ in the believer is seen.

Hannah's story teaches us another important lesson. She was deeply distressed (vv. 7, 10, 15), but she portrays vividly the experience we go through before finding peace and strength in the Lord Jesus. In any difficulty, there is always the temptation to solve our own problems. In today's world, people are encouraged to be independent and to stand on their own two feet, to be assertive and to fight their own battles – to look after ourselves. As Christians, we should indeed be people who can meet our own responsibilities, but we do this under the Lord's direction and with His help. The Lord Jesus was the most powerful man who ever walked on this earth, but He never did anything without reference to His Father in heaven. He spent early mornings and late nights praying over the work He came to do. The Lord's pattern of life is vital to the Christian. When problems arise, we take them to the Lord in prayer and in the light of His word. We do not try to solve them in our own strength. Peter tried this approach and ended up denying the Lord Jesus. Hannah couldn't change her circumstances, but her distress drove her to the Lord.

However, Elkanah, although he deeply loved his wife, did not understand the distress she was experiencing. He tried to remove it. In verse 8 he made the classic mistake of overestimating his own importance: "Am I not better to you than ten sons?" Sometimes husbands, even the most loving Christian husbands, can be over-simplistic in their reactions to the needs of their wives. Just to say, "It's OK" is not enough. The Lord's compassion brings Him into our circumstances. It is this compassion towards each other that should be seen in our marriages. Elkanah did not feel his wife's pain in his heart and, consequently, was insensitive to her deep distress.

Christian husbands should never overvalue themselves. We must not dismiss the needs and experiences our wives can go through, and certainly not address them in terms of our own importance. A better response would have been for Elkanah to share the sorrow of His wife; in the words of Romans 12:15, to "weep with those who weep". He should have supported her spiritually by understanding the situation and his inability to solve it. She should not have had to go to the House of God alone. He should have been by her side. In all relationships, we can be examples, but we are not solutions. We are to be sensitive to the needs of others, especially of those closest to us, and direct them to the Lord Jesus. There is no doubt Elkanah loved his wife. But at this point in their relationship his love was not intelligent or compassionate. This was to change!

Day 11

Hannah's prayer

And Hannah was in bitterness of soul, and prayed to
the Lord and wept in anguish. (1 Samuel 1:10)

Hannah's distress led her, not to despair, but to action. Never allow distressing circumstances to drive you to despair, but to the Throne of Grace. If Hannah's life teaches us anything, it is how to pray. She gives us a pattern for a powerful prayer life. James teaches us how effective, fervent prayer has profound results (James 5:16). Hannah proved this.

Hannah prayed righteously. We cannot expect God to answer our prayers if our lives are not righteous. Christians are to live lives characterised by righteousness, not self-righteousness, but orderly obedient lives directed by the word of God.

Hannah prayed effectively and fervently. She felt deeply about what she was praying for. In Luke 22:44 the Lord Jesus prays "more fervently" (NLT). I have to confess my prayers can lack this deep feeling and concern.

Hannah prayed with tears. Her emotions were affected, not in a sentimental way, but because she was praying for something she felt deeply in her heart and which meant so much to her.

Hannah prayed specifically. She did not waste words. Her distress produced a simplicity and clarity of thought in the presence of God. In her humility there was confidence. In Matthew 6:7 the Lord Jesus reminds us not to be characterised by vain repetition and many words. It was said of Samuel, Hannah's son, that the Lord "let none of his words fall to the ground" (1 Samuel 3:19). Samuel was directed by the Lord before he spoke, and when he spoke, he spoke clearly and wisely. Today we live in the age of the throwaway line. Often words are spoken without real meaning or sincerity. We should not speak to God or to each other in that way, but with true hearts.

Hannah prayed sacrificially. Someone wisely said, "Pray as though nothing depended on you and work as though everything depended on you." Hannah counted the cost. She knew only God could answer her prayer, but she was prepared to sacrifice what would be her greatest joy (v. 11). If we expect God to answer our prayers, we should be willing to yield all we have to Him in sacrificial service.

Hannah prayed silently. Audible prayer is not necessarily powerful prayer. God looks on our hearts. Many years later the Lord sent Samuel to the house of Jesse to anoint a king to replace Saul. Jesse was David's father. Jesse lined up his sons. David was absent and looking after his father's sheep. He was not considered important enough to be present. When Samuel saw Jesse's sons, powerful, attractive men as they all were, he thought, "Surely God would choose one of them to be king of Israel"; just as Israel had chosen Saul, a man head and shoulders above anyone else in the land. God spoke to His old servant and reminded him that God does not look on the outward appearance but upon the heart (1 Samuel 16:7). He taught him a lesson in old age which his mother had learned before Samuel was born; a lesson we easily forget. We, too, are tricked into thinking that what is seen and heard is the most important. Hannah spoke in her heart and it was from there her voice was heard. God never stops listening to our hearts.

Day 12

Thursday

Hannah's peace

Hannah "went her way and ate, and her face was no longer sad."
(1 Samuel 1:18)

Eli was the High Priest when Hannah lived. He was a tragic failure, and his sons were the most corrupt men. Paul reminds us in 1 Timothy 3:4-5 that anyone who did not rule his own house was not to have a responsible role in the house of God. Eli was judged by God for his failure as a father and a priest (1 Samuel 3:12-14). He held the highest spiritual office in the kingdom but totally lacked spiritual discernment. He completely misinterpreted Hannah's distress. And, in doing so, added to it. Godly behaviour is often misunderstood, even by those who are in a position to know better. It was the Chief Priests and Scribes who led the way in judging and ultimately crucifying the Lord of Glory. We should not be surprised if, in being faithful to the Lord Jesus, criticism and even persecution follow.

Hannah defended herself in a very touching way, explaining that she had "poured out" her soul before the Lord (v. 15). In 1 Peter 5:6-7 we read, "Humble yourselves, therefore, under the mighty hand of God, that He may exalt you in due time, casting all your care upon Him; for He cares for you." Hannah was to learn how true this was, and so can we. The words of Hebrews 4:16 encourage us to "come boldly unto the throne of grace that we may obtain mercy and find grace to help in time of need." God responds to those who approach Him in simple faith, bringing their needs to the One who not only can meet them, but wants to.

Once Eli understood the real situation, he sent Hannah away in peace. At the end of her prayer, she returned home at peace. She ate and was no longer sad. Hannah is a remarkable Old Testament illustration of what Paul writes in Philippians 4:6:7, "Be anxious for nothing: but in everything by prayer and supplication with thanksgiving, let your requests be made known unto God; and the peace of God, which surpasses all understanding, will guard your hearts and minds through Christ Jesus." Real prayer leads to real peace. And there is a time to stop praying and leave things in faith with the Lord.

God was going to transform Hannah's life with the birth of Samuel. But we also have to realise that God may not change our circumstances. Paul prayed three times that God would remove an illness he described as a 'a thorn in his side'. The Lord answered his prayer just as clearly as he answered Hannah prayer. His answer was, "My grace is sufficient for you, for My strength is made perfect in weakness. Therefore most gladly I will rather boast in my infirmities, that the power of Christ may rest upon me" (2 Corinthians 12:9).

Hannah was still a childless woman when she left the house of God, but she was no longer sad. She had placed all her need at the Throne of Grace. God was to answer her with a remarkable child. Paul also left his need at the Throne of Grace. He was content that God would not take away his illness but use it to manifest His grace. These are profound lessons. They shape us into the people God wants us to be, and they make us more Christlike. Hannah was at peace and so was Paul because they had been in the presence of the God of peace.

Day 13

Friday

Hannah, a worshipper

So Hannah conceived and bore a son, and called his name Samuel, saying, "Because I have asked for him from the LORD."
(*1 Samuel 1:20*)

Hannah's prayer was answered. God remembered Hannah and she bore a son, whom she called Samuel. Names in the Bible are very instructive and Samuel means "Heard by God", a simple testimony to what God had done. In our own marriage we got to a point where we did not think we would have children. Like many other couples we had thought we would have children without any difficulty. Happily, in God's grace and time, He gave us a daughter. We called her Anna Sarah, and because our surname began with "K", her initials were "ASK". She is a constant reminder to us of God's ability to meet our deepest desires if it is His will.

It is interesting that Hannah, like Elizabeth the mother of John the Baptist in Luke 1:60, took the lead in giving the child his name. Both Hannah and Elizabeth had key roles in the spiritual development of their children. In 2 Timothy 1:5 Paul reminds Timothy of the spiritual influence of Timothy's grandmother, Lois, and his mother, Eunice. The influence of a godly mother on the spiritual welfare of her children cannot be over emphasised. It should not be allowed to be minimised by the pressures of living in today's world.

But Hannah did have to sacrifice. The time came when she had to give up her child to God as she promised. It is wonderful to see the way in which Elkanah supports her in what must have been a most testing time in her life. Hannah could have been tempted to keep Samuel and to spiritualise the vow she made. Elkanah supported his wife nursing Samuel, but gently reminds Hannah, "Only let the LORD establish His word" (v. 23). Elkanah had learned from the experiences God had taken them through. He was no longer insensitive to his wife's needs, but supported her in the sacrifice she was about to make. She returned to the house of God with her loving husband by her side. They worshipped as a family and brought their child to Eli. This act of utter faith in God is very powerful. Samuel was to be left in the care of Eli, a man who had failed God so seriously and the head of a corrupt priesthood. Yet Hannah trusts God to keep and to bless her son. Christian parents need the same kind of faith when the time comes for their children to face a world where there are so many spiritual, moral and physical dangers. This is the time when we need to pray and act constantly for the good of our children, now out of our immediate care.

Hannah and Elkanah learned that God was sovereign and loving. He had led His people to the bitter waters of Marah and changed them into sweet waters (Exodus 15:22-25). They would never have known the richness of God's blessing without knowing what it was to walk with Him through the pain and distress of the experiences He had allowed. In the same way, in the bitter experiences we have as believers, our "Marahs" are transformed when Christ's love and grace are applied to such circumstances. Hannah's godliness profoundly affected her husband Eli, her son Samuel, ultimately, through Samuel, resulting in the blessing of the nation of Israel. Never let us underestimate the value of one person's experience with God, nor fail to see how God can use bitter experiences to lead us into marvellous blessing. "My God shall supply all your need according to His riches in glory by Christ Jesus" (Philippians 4:19).

Our God has not changed!

Day 14

Saturday

Willing to come near

"How often I wanted to gather your children together, as a hen gathers her chicks under her wings, but you were not willing!"

(Matthew 23:37)

After a fierce forest fire, some exhausted fire-fighters were walking back to their vehicles through the burnt ground of what had been a farmyard. One of them noticed something sticking up from the field and, as he passed by, he kicked over the unusual charred remains. To his complete surprise, underneath the object he had kicked away were three or four little chicks, still alive. The charred remains were all that was left of their mother. As the fire had raged, the mother hen gathered her chicks and waited for the flames to pass, as she protected her brood under her wings. Astonishingly the tiny chicks had been saved.

Several times in the Old Testament wings are used to illustrate God's constant care and protection for His people – His desire to keep them close. In Deuteronomy 32:10-11 eagle's wings are used to describe how God carried His people through the wilderness:

> "He kept him as the apple of his eye.
> As an eagle stirs up its nest,
> Hovers over its young,
> Spreading out its wings, taking them up,
> Carrying them on its wings."

When Boaz, King David's great-grandfather, first met Ruth, his future wife, he encouraged her by saying, "The Lord repay your work, and a full reward be given you by the Lord God of Israel, under whose wings you have come for refuge" (Ruth 2:12).

As Jesus experienced the rejection of His people, He looked over Jerusalem and expressed the feelings of His heart with these words, "How often I wanted to gather your children together, as a hen gathers her chicks under her wings, but you were not willing!" (Matthew 23:37). Jesus said, "But you were not willing." Of course, He was talking about a rebellious nation. But all of us are capable of drifting away from our Saviour. The Ephesians, for all their spiritual blessings, lost their first love. This doesn't necessarily mean we stop participating in all the aspects of Christian fellowship. It means, as our hearts grow cold, we lose the joy of our salvation and we go through the motions. Throughout the history of Christendom there has been the constant danger of rebellion against the centrality of Christ and the simplicity of following Him.

In Genesis, Joseph beautifully illustrates the heart of Christ when He said to his brothers, "Come near to me" (Genesis 45:4). Barnabas gave the finest spiritual advice to the young Christians at Antioch when he "exhorted them all, that with purpose of heart they would cleave unto the Lord" (Acts 11:23, KJV). The word "cleave" means to join or glue together. Barnabas was saying to those believers, 'Above all else stay close to the Lord.' This vital, simple exhortation has never lost its relevance. There is no safer place or more powerful place than being close to the Lord. Although there are many reasons why we cease to have fellowship with our Saviour, He never loses the desire to bring us into the blessing of His presence. His love never fails. The important thing is to face up to the things that separate us from the enjoyment of this love, then be willing to open our hearts and know again the peace and safety of sheltering beneath the grace and love of God.

Day 15

Sunday

My Shepherd

The LORD is my shepherd; I shall not want. (Psalm 23:1)

In six short verses Psalm 23 brings home to us so many vital spiritual blessings which always fill our hearts with the wonder of God's salvation. The Psalm begins with the *Person* of the Shepherd. David must have often looked up at night to see the star-filled sky and to worship God as the Creator. At the same time, he knew that glorious Person as his Shepherd. This filled his heart with holy confidence: "I shall not want." He knew that God was the source of every spiritual and material blessing.

David applies his experience as a shepherd to his own spiritual experience when he writes about the *Pastures* of the Shepherd (v.2). David understood the importance of fellowship with God, and he teaches us a fundamental lesson. We think of communion as something we initiate. But David saw it as something God initiates. The Lord wants to have fellowship with us, and He leads us into His presence. Communion is essential to discipleship and being in the presence of God is restorative.

David then writes about the *Paths* of the Shepherd (v. 3). We are empowered to follow the Shepherd in righteousness, to witness to Him. God has a pathway of righteousness for each of us. There are things we experience which are familiar to us all, but we also need personal direction and guidance. This leading is needed each day.

We are not exempt from the dangers of this world or the circumstances of life. But our times are in His hand. Peter,

James and John were the Lord's closest disciples. Their rich spiritual experience of the Lord was of enormous benefit to the Church of God. Why was Peter rescued from Herod? Why was James executed? (Acts 12). We don't know. But we do know the *Presence* of the Shepherd (v. 4). We have His presence throughout our discipleship. Peter experienced this as he slept in his prison cell between the soldiers. And I am sure James experienced it as he was executed by Herod. God's presence is not passive, but is characterised by His pastoral care. His rod guides us, and His staff comforts us.

In verse 5 David writes of the *Provision* of the Shepherd. We have the fellowship of the Shepherd in a world which is often hostile to our faith in Christ. We are in the world but not of it, and the Great Shepherd provides all that we need. The key to this is the blessing of the Spirit of God, the anointing (1 John 2:20). And our blessing is intended to overflow and reach out to others.

Finally, we have the *Promise* of the Shepherd (v. 6). David traces God's goodness in joyous times, and God's mercy in times of need. The Shepherd's presence is forever: "I will never leave you nor forsake you" (Hebrews 13:5). And He promises to bring us into the Father's house (John 14:1-3).

This morning, as we come together, may our hearts be filled with worship to the Good Shepherd.

Day 16

Happy Monday!

And whatever you do, do it heartily, as to the Lord and not to men, knowing that from the Lord you will receive the reward of the inheritance; for you serve the Lord Christ.

(Colossians 3:23-24)

Another Monday morning! This is usually the day when the working week begins. If we like our work, we look forward to Mondays. If we don't, it can be hard to start the week. The Lord Jesus spent the greater part of His life working in obscurity as a tradesman. During this period, we are told He grew in favour with God and man (Luke 2:52). Part of His preparation for public ministry was submitting Himself to the rigours of working life. Mark calls Him "the carpenter" (Mark 6:3). He is also called the "carpenter's son" (Matthew 13:55). Not only did the Lord Jesus work with His hands, but He knew what it was like to work for someone else. The whole of His life on earth was lived in obedience to His Father. He said He always did those things which please the Father (see John 8:29). Doing this involved working for Joseph in all the quietness and ordinariness of Nazareth.

Many people view their jobs only as a means of making a living – the "I work to live, not live to work" approach. There is a disconnect between their work and the rest of their lives. As Christians, we can also divorce our work from our faith, rather than embracing it as a means of expressing our faith. It does have challenges. Just as we cannot choose our relatives when we marry, we can rarely select the people we work with or the people we work for. In his writings Paul introduces a principle of work for the Christian. It is a principle you will not find in any industrial relations legislation. And it is a simple principle: we work for the Lord. It is an ancient principle. We see vivid illustrations of it in the lives of Joseph, Ruth and Daniel, men and women of God who worked with dignity and joyfulness in the most trying of circumstances. My father was not a Christian, but he was a man whose example of uncomplaining hard work, honesty and care for his family left a lasting impression on me.

Paul was a highly intelligent, highly educated and extraordinarily gifted man of God, and he was also a tentmaker. He didn't live in a spiritual bubble. His tentmaking brought him into contact with everyday life. He said to the Ephesian elders, "Yes, you yourselves know that these hands have provided for my necessities, and for those who were with me. I have shown you in every way, by labouring like this, that you must support the weak" (Acts 20:34-35).

People approach work in different ways. Some people are lazy, others hard working. Some complain endlessly, others love to work. Some are only motivated by money, others by vocation. Some scheme to climb the career ladder in any way they can, others are responsible and considerate. But Paul, as always, brings before us the Lord Jesus, and he simply encourages us to work for Him with all our hearts. And he assures us of the Lord's personal reward for displaying His Lordship in our daily work.

Happy Monday morning!

Day 17

Time

To everything there is a season,
A time for every purpose under heaven:
A time to be born,
And a time to die;
A time to plant,
And a time to pluck what is planted. (Ecclesiastes 3:1-2)

The human heart is an incredible organ. By the time you are sixty-six years old, it will have completed around two and a half billion beats. What is also astonishing is that your heart begins to beat twenty-one days after you are conceived in your mother's womb! Heartbeats mark the passage of time. Each second, minute, hour, day, month and year can never be repeated. They mark out the unique journey we take through life and measure our days.

The writer of Ecclesiastes takes up the subject of time. He begins, "To everything there is a season, a time for every purpose under heaven." We associate seasons – spring, summer, autumn, winter – with nature. The cycle of life is expressed in birth and development, maturity and fruitfulness, ageing and finally death. What we see in nature, we also see in our human experience. The writer of Ecclesiastes understood this pattern, and he understood human experience.

But the Bible brings in another dimension: the spiritual dimension. Ecclesiastes teaches that there is a time for everything; also that there is a purpose to everything. God allows us to pass through a whole range of experiences, but these are not random or accidental. They have both meaning and purpose. "And we know that all things work together for good to those who love God, to those who are the called according to His purpose" (Romans 8:28).

The beginning and ending of life is highlighted in verse 2: "A time to be born, and a time to die; a time to plant, and a time to pluck what is planted." This verse sets the two boundaries of human life: the "time to be born" and the "time to die". And it also implies a harvest when the value of a life is realised. The writer paints a picture of a farmer planting a seed and later receiving a harvest. It is beautiful to see God as the farmer, the seed as our life and the harvest as our death. It is not merely that life begins and ends, but that it has a purpose, to produce fruit for God: "By this My Father is glorified, that you bear much fruit; so you will be My disciples (John15:8).

The Lord Jesus uses the same illustration of planting and harvest to describe His own experience of life, death and resurrection: "Jesus answered them, saying, 'The hour has come that the Son of Man should be glorified. Most assuredly, I say to you, unless a grain of wheat falls into the ground and dies, it remains alone; but if it dies, it produces much grain'" (John 12:23-24). The Eternal Son of God entered into time and passed through the cycle of natural life that we experience. He describes His perfect work of salvation in terms of a grain of wheat, planted in death and bringing a glorious harvest in resurrection. Our lives for Him follow the same pattern. We have received life in Him. It has brought us into fellowship with God and given us the capacity to live fruitful lives for Him. We possess eternal life. We enjoy it now, and we will enter into all its fullness in a coming eternal day.

The question is, How do we use the time we have in response to the Saviour who lived and died and lives again for us?

Day 18

A time to destroy and a time to build

A time to kill,
And a time to heal;
A time to break down,
And a time to build up;
A time to weep,
And a time to laugh;
A time to mourn,
And a time to dance.   *(Ecclesiastes 3:3-4)*

In verse 3 killing and demolition are contrasted with healing and construction. There are times when in order to build up we have to destroy. This concept is not foreign to the New Testament. In Colossians 3:5 Paul writes, "Therefore put to death your members which are on the earth: fornication, uncleanness, passion, evil desire, and covetousness, which is idolatry." He identifies those things which emerge from our own hearts to endanger our spiritual welfare and destroy our testimony. There is only one way to deal with them and that is to put them to death. We can't alter the flesh in us. God doesn't change our old lives: He gives us new life. That's why Paul then writes, "Therefore, as the elect of God, holy and beloved, put on tender mercies, kindness, humility, meekness, longsuffering; bearing with one another, and forgiving one another, if anyone has a complaint against another; even as Christ forgave you, so you also must do. But above all these things put on love, which is the bond of perfection" (Colossians 3:12-14).

It is so vital to have the spiritual resolve to destroy the evil influences which confront us and always to encourage what is of God. Life is about choices. These choices either damage us or lead us into blessing. David looked at Bathsheba (2 Samuel 11:2-3). In that moment, instead of putting to death the lust that arose in his heart, he decided to do what he knew was wrong. This led to untold misery. We can be profoundly affected by the decisions we take in one moment of time. The prodigal son came to a critical moment in his life when he said to himself, "I will arise and go to my father." That would be a difficult journey to make. But what did he do? He got up and went back to his father. He made a decision which led to healing and blessing (Luke15:18-20).

In verse 4 the subjects of joy and sorrow are addressed. These extremes are an integral part of our lives. As Christians, we are not exempt from times of failure, disappointment, sadness, pain and illness; times when we weep. Also, bereavement; times when we mourn. And there are the joyous times of salvation, love, fellowship, friendships, service, marriage, and parenthood. We enjoy the spiritual and material blessings of God in our own lives and share in those of others. These are times when joy fills our whole being. Joyful and sorrowful times are part of our lives what is important is how we learn from these experiences. Do we enjoy our times of blessings, selfishly? Do we allow difficulties to embitter us? Or do we share the joyous times God gives us and allow the times of suffering to shape us into compassionate, understanding and Christlike people?

Let love be without hypocrisy. Abhor what is evil. Cling to what is good. Be kindly affectionate to one another with brotherly love, in honour giving preference to one another; not lagging in diligence, fervent in spirit, serving the Lord; rejoicing in hope, patient in tribulation, continuing steadfastly in prayer; distributing to the needs of the saints, given to hospitality. Bless those who persecute you; bless and do not curse. Rejoice with those who rejoice, and weep with those who weep (Romans 12:9-15).

Day 19

A time to gain and a time to lose

A time to cast away stones,
And a time to gather stones;
A time to embrace,
And a time to refrain from embracing;
A time to gain,
And a time to lose;
A time to keep,
And a time to throw away.   *(Ecclesiastes 3:5-6)*

Stones are often referred to in the Bible. There were the great stones used to build the Temple. And Peter uses the illustration "living stones" to describe the members of Christ's Church. But in our verse, stones are looked at as pictures of what can be a hindrance to us, or a help. We can accumulate habits and occupations which clutter our lives and make our spiritual journey more difficult. The Lord tells us about stony ground (Matthew 13:5), where there is not enough depth of soil for the seed to grow. And it has an application in our lives as Christians. It is not that what we occupy ourselves with is bad; the question is whether it has value. Does it help or does it hinder our spiritual progress and witness for the Lord Jesus? To do this we need to build into our lives "precious stones" (1 Corinthians 3:12) – communion with Christ, prayer, obedience to the word of God, fellowship with God's people and simply doing good.

Equally, there are times when it is legitimate to enjoy intimacy, "a time to embrace". And on the other hand, there are times when we need to be free to get on and do things. The Lord gives us an example of this with Mary in John 20. She was overjoyed to see the Lord in resurrection and held on to Him. But the Lord said, "Do not cling to Me, for I have not yet ascended to My Father; but go to My brethren and say to them, 'I am ascending to My Father and your Father, and to My God and your God'" (John 20:17). It was not that He did not value her affection, but there were things to do.

This theme is continued in verse 6: "A time to gain, and a time to lose; a time to keep, and a time to throw away". In the Gospels the Lord Jesus constantly reminds us of the importance of this process. In regard to salvation He says, "For what profit is it to a man if he gains the whole world, and loses his own soul? Or what will a man give in exchange for his soul?" (Matthew 16:26). In the previous verse, the Lord Jesus says, "For whoever desires to save his life will lose it, but whoever loses his life for My sake will find it" (Matthew 16:25). He uses a similar expression in all the Gospels (see Mark 8:35, Luke 9:24 and John 12:25), emphasising how important this concept is to salvation and discipleship. The Christian pathway on the one hand involves sacrifice, but on the other enjoys the gain of spiritual blessing.

Paul describes his own discipleship in terms of losing and gaining. "But what things were gain to me, these I have counted loss for Christ" (Philippians 3:7). He also describes in terms of "great gain" the peace of walking with God and the experience of contentment: "Now godliness with contentment is great gain" (1 Timothy 6:6). This pattern of losing and gaining is further emphasised in Philippians 4:11-12: "Not that I speak in regard to need, for I have learned in whatever state I am, to be content." People seek gain, and fear being identified as a "loser". In Christ we learn the blessing of gaining and the blessing of losing.

Day 20

A time to tear and a time to sew

A time to tear,
And a time to sew;
A time to keep silence,
And a time to speak. (Ecclesiastes 3:7)

The tearing of clothes was a practice in the Old Testament that was a sign of repentance. For example, it says of Ezra, "At the evening sacrifice I arose from my fasting; and having torn my garment and my robe, I fell on my knees and spread out my hands to the LORD my God" (Ezra 9:5). To repent is not merely feeling sorry for what we have done wrong; it involves doing something about it. It means to change for the better. The physical act of tearing one's clothes expressed the genuineness of a repentant heart. It was an expression of failure and dependence upon God's mercy and a desire to be clothed anew in His righteousness.

Sewing is about repairing and gives the sense that what was torn was of value. I remember when I was a child watching my grandmother darning socks which had become worn. She would say there was no shame in a darned sock, only in a sock with a hole in it. We live in a "throw-away" society. Often it is not worth repairing something because it is cheaper to buy another product. Thankfully we do not yet think of fellow human beings in those terms. We naturally seek to do all we can to heal sickness and disease, and everything will be done to save a life.

The Bible also refers to spiritual healing. At the outset of His public ministry, Jesus read out:

"The Spirit of the LORD is upon Me,
Because He has anointed Me
To preach the gospel to the poor;
He has sent Me to heal the broken-hearted" (Luke
4:18, from Isaiah 61:1).

Paul highlights the importance of restoring or healing those who have made mistakes: "Brethren, if a man is overtaken in any trespass, you who are spiritual restore such a one in a spirit of gentleness, considering yourself lest you also be tempted" (Galatians 6:1). This ministry of restoration is essential to Christian fellowship.

The writer of Ecclesiastes places "a time to keep silence" before "a time to speak". James has a similar thought: "So then, my beloved brethren, let every man be swift to hear, slow to speak." James 1:19. The Lord Jesus preached and taught for three years, but during His trial He kept silent. Isaiah describes Him:

… as a sheep before its shearers is silent,
So He opened not His mouth (Isaiah 53:7).

At times, the wisest course of action is to remain silent. Often our words can add fuel to the fire. Throughout history, men have used the power of speech to inflame peoples' passions and persuaded them to follow a path that caused the world great harm. The tongue, as James reminds us, is a small part of the body but capable of doing untold damage.

On the other hand, there are times when we need to speak "the truth in love" (Ephesians 4:15), and we must speak. When a friend, at some personal cost, speaks to us in love to point out things which may be painful but are right, we need the grace to accept what is said. "Faithful are the wounds of a friend" (Proverbs 27:6). In doing so, it is extraordinary to discover that God uses such "wounds" to bring about spiritual blessing.

Day 21

Saturday

A time to love and and a time to hate

A time to love,
And a time to hate;
A time of war,
And a time of peace. *(Ecclesiastes 3:8)*

Psalm 45:7 says prophetically of Christ, "You love righteousness and hate wickedness." Isaiah warns of those who "call evil good and good evil" (see Isaiah 5:20). It is a dangerous moral path we tread when we overlook what is evil and, even worse, convince ourselves it is good. Undermining good by portraying it as evil is a sign of moral bankruptcy. The Christian should never be surprised by the contortions of the human mind when it attempts to justify moral failure. Our testimony is to follow our Saviour by loving righteousness and hating wickedness.

This process is described as a war in Ephesians 6. To be victorious, we find our strength in the Lord and in the indwelling power of the Holy Spirit. And we are given the whole armour of God to fight the spiritual battle we are in (see Ephesians 6:10-18). The writer of Ecclesiastes finishes this remarkable passage with "a time for peace." It is a fitting end to the insights he brings before us. The Christian has peace with God (Romans 5:1), the Christian enjoys a peace which passes all understanding (Philippians 4:7) and the Christian knows the God of peace (Philippians 4:9). The Lord Jesus is described as the Prince of Peace, and in John 14:27 He says, "Peace I leave with you, My peace I give to you; not as the world gives do I give to you. Let not your heart be troubled, neither let it be afraid." The writer of Ecclesiastes views one time as succeeding another time. But astonishingly, we can know the peace of God's presence at the very time we are passing through circumstances which are anything but peaceful.

Over the past few days we have thought about time. We need time to worship and pray, time to listen to God in His word, time for each other, time for our children, our families, our friends, our fellowship, and our neighbours. We need to sacrifice time in service, but also to "rest a while" (Mark 6:31). We also need to make time to consider the journey we are taking in life. With 24 hours in a day and 7 days in a week, each week has 168 hours. It is good to reflect on how we use this precious resource. We can never go back to reuse time. But by the grace of God, even when we have wasted years, we are never to forget that God has the power to restore to us "the years that the swarming locust has eaten" (Joel 2:25).

Scripture encourages us to reflect and take action regarding our use of time: "Making the best use of time, because the days are evil" (Ephesians 5:16, ESV); "Conduct yourselves wisely towards outsiders, making the best use of time" (Colossians 4:5 ESV). God has given us one life with which to honour Him, and one day that life will be complete. He encourages us to live day by day, using the time given to us wisely and profitably and with the confidence that our "times are in His hand" (Psalm 31:15). John Wesley said, "I am not careful for what may be a hundred years hence. He who governed the world before I was born shall take care of it likewise when I am dead. My part is to improve the present moment."

That present moment is today!

Day 22

Sunday

Laid down

And she brought forth her firstborn Son, and wrapped Him in swaddling cloths, and laid Him in a manger because there was no room for them in the inn. (Luke 2:7)

Now in the place where He was crucified there was a garden, and in the garden a new tomb in which no one had yet been laid. So there they laid Jesus, because of the Jews' Preparation Day, for the tomb was nearby. (John 19:41-42)

Luke uniquely records the birth of Jesus Christ. He beautifully describes the coming of the Saviour into the world. Mary, after giving birth, wrapped her child and laid Him in a manger. When we read of that tender moment, it is easy for us to overlook the immense power of God at work. A few verses later, heaven responds to the birth of Jesus Christ. The angel speaks of the all-powerful Saviour being born: "Christ the Lord". But he presents this glorious person as a "babe wrapped in swaddling cloths, lying in a manger" (Luke 2:12). There is nothing more helpless or dependent than a newborn baby. We should never cease to wonder at the incarnation. God reveals the immensity of His eternal love and power in the tininess of Immanuel.

In John 10 the Lord Jesus speaks of Himself as the Good Shepherd and of laying down His life for the sheep. That laying down was to mean crucifixion. This means of execution slowly ended the lives of those who endured such awful suffering, while enemies mocked and loved ones were left broken hearted. The world sought to take everything away from the Lord, even His clothes. But Calvary is not only about what man, energised by Satan, takes away. It is about what the Lord Jesus holds: "I have power to lay it down" (John 10:18).

Joseph of Arimathea asked for the body of Jesus and "he took it down, wrapped it in linen, and laid it in a tomb that was hewn out of the rock, where no one had ever lain before" (Luke 23:53). Death and the grave appear at this time to display their sting and victory over the Lord of life. But Jesus destroys the power of death: "I have power to take it again" (John 10:18). As the Apostle Paul writes: "Death is swallowed up in victory."

> "O Death, where is your sting?
> O Hades, where is your victory?"
> The sting of death is sin, and the strength of sin is the law. But thanks be to God, who gives us the victory through our Lord Jesus Christ (1 Corinthians 15:54-57).

The Lord's birth, life, death and consequently His resurrection are characterised by the wonder of His "laying down", the love displayed in the giving of Himself.

It was this love that caused the people of God to experience being of "one heart and one soul" and to lay down their resources in sacrifice to God as the Church of Christ began to grow (Acts 4:32-37). It is the same love that stimulates our worship and sacrificial service for the Lord: "By this we know love, because He laid down His life for us. And we also ought to lay down our lives for the brethren" (1 John 3:16).

Day 23

Monday

Joseph, the husband of Mary

Now the birth of Jesus Christ was as follows: After His mother Mary was betrothed to Joseph, before they came together, she was found with child of the Holy Spirit.　　　　(Matthew 1:18)

Joseph is one of the most overlooked men in the Bible. He was a carpenter, whose voice we never hear but whom God chose to be the guardian of His Son Jesus Christ. Matthew takes time in the first chapter of his Gospel to trace the genealogy of Jesus Christ. The genealogy highlights two great men of renown. The first is David, the shepherd boy who saved his nation and became their greatest king. The second is Abraham, the great man of faith, and "the friend of God". Matthew traces the lineage of Jesus Christ from Abraham to Joseph. In this genealogy we can also reflect upon the failure of two great men of faith, Judah and David, and the faith of two remarkable women, Rahab and Ruth. God does not hide His people's sinfulness, but demonstrates His ability through grace to bring good out of evil. God does not excuse evil, as David discovered, but evil never confounds the purposes of God. The genealogy goes on to the division of the kingdom of Israel during the reign of Rehoboam and then the nation's gradual decline. This decline eventually led to Judah going into captivity in Babylon. Although the exiles returned to Israel, the royal line ended in the obscurity and the poverty of Nazareth, where we discover Joseph.

Verse 16 introduces Joseph as "the husband of Mary, of whom was born Jesus who is called Christ." Matthew's account of the birth of Jesus starts with the betrothal of Mary and Joseph (v. 18). Betrothal means to promise "by one's truth". it was an engagement to be married. In New Testament times this took place at least a year before marriage. Betrothal is used to beautifully describe the spiritual relationship between God and His people in the Old Testament: "I will betroth you to Me forever" (read Hosea 2:19-20).

I think Matthew emphasises the betrothal of Mary and Joseph, not only as a fact but also to introduce us to a man of faith, Joseph. His actions illustrate the loving-kindness, mercy, and faithfulness to the God described by Hosea. The plain fact of the matter was that Mary was pregnant. The only conclusion was that she had become pregnant by another man. There was no other possibility, naturally speaking. Luke 1:26-38 gives us the details of how Mary became the mother of Jesus. But Luke doesn't record the distress Joseph goes through when he found out that the woman he loved and was to marry was pregnant. In this distress we see the qualities of Joseph emerge. God would have us pause to reflect on Joseph's character. He was a just, merciful, loving, faithful, obedient, resourceful, hard-working family man who was to become known as the father of Jesus. And he has vital lessons to teach Christian men and husbands.

The first thing Matthew tells us about Joseph was that he was a just man. Joseph wanted to act in the right way. He was not seeking revenge or retribution; he was trying to do God's will in the most difficult of circumstances. So often in such cases, and especially when we feel ourselves to be the wronged party, we are prone to think and act in a self-righteous way. When we find failure in others, it is easy to take the moral high ground and look down on those who have done things we judge to be wrong. The facts about Mary were only known when they were revealed supernaturally. We often make judgments before we know all the facts. This tendency is a very present danger. Joseph had a royal heritage of faith and wisdom, the faith of Abraham, Isaac, Jacob, and David, and the wisdom of Solomon. And he displays that faith and wisdom in true humility.

Day 24

Joseph the man

Because Joseph her husband was faithful to the law, and yet did not want to expose her to public disgrace, he had in mind to divorce her quietly. (Matthew 1:19, NIV)

I remember as a child being told about the capture of Richard the Lionheart. He was caught shortly before Christmas, 1192 at an inn near Vienna. He was discovered because his royal bearing was inconsistent with his lowly disguise. Joseph was a man stripped of all the privileges and blessings of his ancestors, who were kings. Still, his lowliness never disguised his spiritual and moral attributes. It was these attributes that God had always sought in the men who became kings over His people. Many kings, like Herod, were amoral. Joseph shone in the midst of such darkness.

Matthew tells us Joseph was not willing to make Mary a public example. He was not only a just man, but he was a loving and protective man. There is no doubt Joseph loved Mary, and although deeply hurt and confused by the circumstance he was in, he would not harm her. Paul tells us in 1 Corinthians 13:

> Love suffers long and is kind; love does not envy; love does not parade itself, is not puffed up; does not behave rudely, does not seek its own, is not provoked, thinks no evil; does not rejoice in iniquity, but rejoices in the truth; bears all things, believes all things, hopes all things, endures all things (vv. 4-7).

I think Joseph demonstrates these beautiful features of love as he comes to terms with his situation. He sought to protect the woman he believed had betrayed him, by quietly ending their betrothal. There is no sense of rage and revenge in Joseph. He had a quietness of spirit and a desire to act protectively and discreetly. Discretion is not greatly valued in our society today. The private lives of people are broadcast in the most detailed way. Nothing is left to the imagination. But Solomon, one of Joseph's greatest ancestors, wrote: "Hatred stirs up strife,/But love covers all sins" (Proverbs 10:12) and "He who covers a transgression seeks love,/But he who repeats a matter separates friends" (Proverbs 17:9).

Joseph sought to deal with problems in the most thoughtful and caring way. He gave significant consideration to the situation he and Mary faced. Joseph didn't rush into a decision. And once he had clarified what he was going to do, he continued to reflect on it before taking action. His actions speak volumes about his character. He wanted the best possible outcomes for Mary and himself. It is so important as Christians that we learn from this process. Decision-making is a vital issue, and we should reflect in the presence of God on the steps we take before rushing into action. Reflection is critical because it allows time to review our thought-processes and for God to direct us along the path He wants us to take. This is especially important when our decisions affect the lives of others.

Joseph's story also shows how God exercises Joseph's faith and then intervenes to explain what he did not know. The concept of "waiting upon the Lord" is woven throughout the Old Testament. It describes the habit of going into the presence of God in prayer, committing our way to Him, and waiting for His direction. In the words of Proverbs 3:5-6:

> Trust in the LORD with all your heart,
> And lean not on your own understanding;
> In all your ways acknowledge Him,
> And He shall direct your paths.

God was about to respond to Joseph's faithfulness.

Day 25

Joseph the husband

Then Joseph, being aroused from sleep, did as the angel of the Lord commanded him and took to him his wife, and did not know her till she had brought forth her firstborn Son. And he called His name Jesus.　(Matthew 1:24-25)

God spoke to Joseph through a dream. Today we have the whole of the Bible and the indwelling Holy Spirit to direct and guide us in our daily lives. But God still exercises our faith to learn what it means to live in accord with His will for us. The will of God includes what is common to all the children of God and what is specific to our personal lives. In a world and a society resistant to the claims of Christ we are constantly challenged to live for Him in difficult circumstances. Joseph's example encourages us to be just, loving, merciful, thoughtful, patient, and reflective in the steps of faith. His story also teaches us that the Lord will make clear to us the path He wants us to take, if we seek His presence.

The angel of the Lord directed Joseph in the most precise way: "Joseph, son of David, do not be afraid to take to you Mary your wife, for that which is conceived in her is of the Holy Spirit. And she will bring forth a Son, and you shall call His name Jesus, for He will save His people from their sins" (vv. 20-21).

He begins by reminding Joseph who he was – "the son of David". Sometimes when we come into God's presence, we do so with a genuine sense of our unworthiness. But God always reminds us of our position before Him in Christ. He assures us of our dignity in Christ. Joseph was a carpenter. But he stood before God as a son of the great king David. And, as with David, God wasn't looking on the outward appearance, He was looking on the heart of this lowly man of God (see 1 Samuel 16:6-7).

The angel lifts an immense load from Joseph's heart by explaining the miraculous event in Mary's life. She was to be the mother of the Saviour of the world. Joseph was told to call the child "Jesus", for He would save His people from their sins. Joseph must have experienced such joy and peace as he heard the words of the angel. All doubt about Mary's faithfulness was removed. Joseph knew she would be the mother of the Messiah, and that he had the responsibility of being a guardian of the Saviour of the world.

In verse 22 Matthew explains that this revelation was a fulfilment of what God had promised to do 700 years before, "Therefore the Lord Himself will give you a sign: Behold, the virgin shall conceive and bear a Son, and you shall call His name Immanuel" (Isaiah 7:14). Time never weakens the promises of God.

At the end of the chapter, Joseph awakes from his sleep and begins immediately to take up his responsibilities. In obedience, he marries Mary and waits for the birth of her Son. When the Saviour is born, it is Joseph who calls Him Jesus. What an example of waiting on the Lord, being assured of His will and then doing it without hesitation!

Day 26

Joseph a father

And it came to pass in those days, that there went out a decree from Caesar Augustus that all the world should be taxed. (And this taxing was first made when Cyrenius was governor of Syria.) And all went to be taxed, everyone into his own city. And Joseph also went up from Galilee, out of the city of Nazareth, into Judaea, unto the city of David, which is called Bethlehem; (because he was of the house and lineage of David:) to be taxed with Mary his espoused wife, being great with child.

(Luke 2:1-5, AV)

It is remarkable to see how God fulfils His prophecy that the Saviour would be born in Bethlehem. Joseph was key to this fulfilment.

Joseph was the lowly relative at the end of a long line of kings. He came from King David's city, Bethlehem, and, in a stable, he witnessed the birth of the Saviour of the world. As a descendant of King David, Joseph was there to welcome into the world King David's greater Son. He witnessed the Creator of the universe entering His creation. Joseph was there, too, when the shepherds arrived, who were to tell the story of the heavenly host announcing the birth of a Saviour: "For unto you is born this day in the city of David a Saviour, which is Christ the Lord" (Luke 2:11, AV). It is striking that simple local shepherds witnessed the arrival of the Good, the Great, and the Chief Shepherd.

Eight days later Joseph named Jesus, "And when eight days were accomplished for the circumcising of the child, his name was called Jesus, which was so named of the angel before he was conceived in the womb" (Luke 2:21, AV).

Joseph was there with Mary when Simeon, who was told by the Spirit of God that he would not die before he had seen the Lord's Christ, took Jesus in his arms (see Luke 2:28-33). Astonishingly, the One of whom it is said, "and underneath are the everlasting arms" rested in the arms of Simeon. Joseph and Mary were also the subjects of Simeon's blessing, and they also heard Anna, the prophetess, giving thanks to God for their Son. All these occasions of joy verified in Joseph's heart who Jesus was. These events must have encouraged him in his responsibility as the guardian of the Son of God.

This encouragement increased when the wise men arrived in Bethlehem at the house of Joseph and Mary. I suspect the house the wise men entered was very simple, but in that home they fell down and worshipped Jesus (Matthew 2:11). This was further evidence of the glory of Christ. First, Jesus was worshipped by His faithful people, the shepherds, Simeon, and Anna. Then, Joseph received into his home Gentile wise men who worshipped Him before presenting their gifts of gold, frankincense, and myrrh. God ensured His Son was welcomed into the world by men and women of faith. These events confirmed to Joseph and Mary the majesty of the Person who was their child. Joseph began to care for Jesus. It is astonishing that the Person who invites us to cast all our care upon Him (see 1 Peter 5:7) knew what it was to be cared for by this faithful man of God.

Day 27

Friday

Joseph, a home builder

And he (Joseph) came and dwelt in a city called Nazareth, that it might be fulfilled which was spoken by the prophets, "He (Jesus) shall be called a Nazarene". (Matthew 2:23)

After the wise men returned home, Joseph was warned in a second dream to take his family to Egypt (Matthew 2:13-15). Joseph was a remarkable man of faith. He quietly obeys God and protects his family. Joseph had witnessed the incredible story of Christ's entrance into the world. God acted in love and grace. It was while this love and grace were dawning on this world, evil became evident. King Herod, in utter wickedness, slaughtered infants in and around Bethlehem. Joseph fled with Mary and Jesus into Egypt. He stayed there until God told him, in a third dream, that it was safe to return to Israel. Again Joseph immediately responds to God's word and returns to his homeland with Mary and the young Child.

Joseph was always alert to his surroundings and protective of his family. Spiritual alertness is vital in a world where spiritual, psychological, and physical dangers abound. The Lord Jesus instructs us to watch and pray. This instruction means to be alert to dangers and to take action to avoid them for the well-being of ourselves and those we care about. When Joseph learned Herod's son was reigning over his father's territory, he didn't go to Bethlehem. Once more, God responds to Joseph's faith, in a fourth dream, to direct him to Galilee and to the town of Nazareth. Matthew refers to a prophecy saying Jesus would be called a Nazarene (Matthew 2:23).

This prophecy may be a reference to Isaiah 11:1-2:

> There shall come forth a Rod from the stem of Jesse,
> And a Branch shall grow out of his roots.
> The Spirit of the LORD shall rest upon Him,
> The Spirit of wisdom and understanding,
> The Spirit of counsel and might,
> The Spirit of knowledge and of the fear of the LORD.

These verses refer to the Messiah. The Branch in verse 1 is the Hebrew word *netzer*. Commentators think "netzer" and "Nazarene" are connected. Isaiah also writes of the Saviour:

> He grew up before him like a tender shoot,
> And like a root out of dry ground (Isaiah 53:2).

Nazareth became the home of Jesus Christ. When the Lord Jesus emerges out of the obscurity of this town to fulfil His powerful public ministry, Nathaniel said, "Can any good thing come out of Nazareth?" (John 1:46). The place was not held in high regard. But it was the place where the Eternal Son of God, who occupied the centre of heaven, grew up: the home of Joseph, the carpenter.

Luke tells us that Jesus went to Nazareth "...where He had been brought up" (Luke 4:16). The title above the head of Jesus at Calvary was "This is Jesus of Nazareth, the King of the Jews." Peter healed the lame man in Jerusalem with the words, "In the name of Jesus Christ of Nazareth, rise up and walk" (Acts 3:6). Recalling his conversion on the road to Damascus in Acts 22, Paul remembers the words spoken to him from heaven by the resurrected and ascended Christ: "I am Jesus of Nazareth whom you are persecuting."

Jesus was not ashamed of Nazareth and the home of Joseph. It is a constant reminder of the love that brought Him from all the glory of heaven to where we were.

Day 28

Joseph's legacy

Then He went down with them and came to Nazareth, and was subject to them, but His mother kept all these things in her heart. And Jesus increased in wisdom and stature, and in favour with God and men. (Luke 2:51-52)

Each year Joseph and his family travelled from Nazareth to Jerusalem to worship. Luke recorded one visit, when Jesus was twelve years old (Luke 2:41-52). As they returned home, Joseph and Mary thought Jesus was with their relatives, but, after discovering this was not the case, they went back to the capital. After three days of searching, they found Jesus sitting among the doctors, listening to them, and asking questions. Everyone was astonished by His understanding and answers.

Mary said to Jesus, "Son, why have You done this to us? Look, Your father and I have sought You anxiously." Jesus answered, "Why did you seek Me? Did you not know that I must be about My Father's business?" Interestingly, Mary spoke of Joseph as Jesus' father. But Jesus spoke of His Father in heaven. They did not understand what Jesus meant, and Jesus returned with them to Nazareth. He was subject to them, and as He grew up in the home at Nazareth, Jesus is described as increasing in wisdom and stature, and in favour with God and men. That home was the home of Joseph, the carpenter.

When Jesus begins his ministry, one of his first disciples is Philip. Philip immediately finds his friend Nathanael and says to him, "We have found Him of whom Moses in the law, and also the prophets, wrote—Jesus of Nazareth, the son of Joseph."

It is a reference to the dignity of the man who cared for the Son of God. In Matthew 13:55 Jesus is called the "carpenter's son". In Mark 6:3 Jesus is called "the carpenter", so Jesus was not only known as the son of the carpenter but as *the carpenter*. Mark teaches us in his Gospel about Jesus as the servant of God. That service embraced an ordinary manual job. In John 13 Jesus undertakes the task of a household slave when He washes the disciples' feet to teach them lowliness. Never let us underestimate the value of every aspect of service for God, however menial it may be. There is a famous story of President Kennedy when he visited Cape Canaveral. He asked a man what his job was. The man was a cleaner, but he replied to the President, "I'm helping to put a man on the moon." He had an overwhelming sense of being part of a great endeavour. Paul tells us, "You serve the Lord Christ" (Colossians 3:24). Do I have a sense of the greatness of the Person I have the opportunity to serve?

As Joseph completes the service God had given him, he disappears from the pages of the Bible as quietly as he appeared. Some commentators believe he had died by the time Jesus began his ministry. We don't know. But it is incredible to think that day by day for thirty years in the obscurity of Nazareth the Son of God grew up and worked alongside Joseph. In all likelihood, Jesus spent more time with Joseph than anyone else. And it was Joseph, a humble man of royal descent, who was used to give Immanuel the title of "Jesus of Nazareth".

I said at the beginning of this talk that Joseph is one of the most overlooked men in the Bible. I believe we should not continue to overlook the spiritual qualities of the man into whose care God chose to place His Son. We never hear Joseph speak. Joseph's voice is the quiet but powerful voice of humility, faith, goodness, mercy, lovingkindness, obedience, courage, provision, protection, peace, hard work, and sacrifice. These attributes are desperately needed in our world today. And Joseph's life is a challenge to every Christian man.

Day 29

Sunday

The promise of the Saviour's presence

For where two or three are gathered together in My name, I am there in the midst of them. *(Matthew 18:20)*

But the Lord stood with me. *(2 Timothy 4:17)*

Then, the same day at evening, being the first day of the week, when the doors were shut where the disciples were assembled, for fear of the Jews, Jesus came and stood in the midst, and said to them, "Peace be with you." When He had said this, He showed them His hands and His side. Then the disciples were glad when they saw the Lord. *(John 20:19-20)*

Over the past week, fears of the further spread of Covid-19 have increased. Action is being taken to re-impose restrictions to counter this increase. In such circumstances, we can be left doubting if our lives will ever return to normal. We feel so restricted. We can't visit or be close to extended families or neighbours, and we especially feel the limitations imposed on Christian fellowship. I usually travel more than 25,000 miles a year. Since lockdown, it has been 3500 miles. Everything planned in our annual circuit of ministry has been cancelled. But what has been such an encouragement to me is understanding the Lord can never be restricted.

In Matthew 18:20 the Saviour describes the tiniest groups: two or three. And He promises to be in their midst. When we think of this verse, we often think of the smallness of the numbers. However, Matthew 18:20 is not about our smallness, but about the Lord's greatness: the power of His omnipresence. He can embrace all of His people in His love and grace in the same moment. He is simultaneously in the midst of every company gathering simply in His name. He never ceases to be the all-powerful Shepherd of the one flock.

But what if we are not part of the smallest group? What if, this morning, we are entirely isolated – alone. This is what Paul felt when he wrote: "At my first defence no one stood with me, but all forsook me" (2 Timothy 4:16). But then in the very next verse he writes, "But the Lord stood with me." When the Lord says, "I will never leave you nor forsake you" (Hebrews 13:5) He is speaking to every single child of God. We may not be able to enjoy each other's fellowship as we once did, but the Lord comes to where we are. He did that to save us, and He continues to come where we are throughout our lives.

Centuries ago, the disciples were restricted and afraid as they met on the first day of the week behind closed doors. These circumstances did not prevent Jesus from coming to them. He filled their hearts with His peace, the reality of His love, and His joy. This morning, whatever the restrictions placed on us, the Lord wants us to know His presence. He wants His peace to rule in our hearts, and His love, that took Him to Calvary, to overwhelm us with joy and worship. And He wants that to be our experience whether we are alone or gathered in the smallest or largest groups, until the day dawns when He will bring us into His eternal presence.

Day 30

Monday

The God of all grace

But may the God of all grace, who called us to His eternal glory by Christ Jesus, after you have suffered a while, perfect, establish, strengthen, and settle you. To Him be the glory and the dominion forever and ever. Amen. (1 Peter 5:10-11)

Peter's heart was full of worship as he drew his first letter to a close. Like Paul, he could trace the wonder of God's grace in his life and gave God the beautiful title of "the God of all grace". Paul tells us in 2 Corinthians 8:9 how we know that grace: "For you know the grace of our Lord Jesus Christ, that though He was rich, yet for your sakes He became poor, that you through His poverty might become rich." We are given life by God's grace, and we are sustained in that life by the same grace. The flow of grace comes from the God of all grace, through the Saviour who manifested it and the Holy Spirit who ministers it. It is known and enjoyed now and will bring every one of us into His eternal presence, because, in grace, God has "called us to His eternal glory by Christ Jesus." Peter encourages his readers by assuring them that their present sufferings were temporary and would be used by God to "perfect, establish, strengthen, and settle you" (1 Peter 5:10).

I remember being a cub scout when I was very young. We used to get "badges" for doing different tasks. One of the few I can remember was being given a pot of soil and told there was a bulb buried inside. My job was to water it each day or so and leave in a darkened room. Every day before school, I would go and take a look at how my bulb was doing. Every day, all I could see was soil! Then one day the tip of the plant appeared through the surface. I can remember the pleasure I felt as, over the following days, my plant sprang into life. Some suffering is clear to everyone, and those who care for us can respond with compassion. But often, suffering is unseen. Like my plant, it takes place in isolation. I couldn't see the struggle taking place beneath the soil, only the results of life when the plant emerged from its dark home. But the God of all grace is not like other gardeners; He can see what's beneath the soil! His presence can be known in the darkness we endure. He completes the work of grace in our hearts. Plants are hardened off in pots, to be taken out and established and strengthened in a garden. Peter was fulfilling the ministry the Lord had given him: "But I have prayed for you, Simon, that your faith may not fail. And when you have turned back, strengthen your brothers" (Luke 22:32, NIV).

Peter encouraged his readers to patiently go through the trials of life knowing the presence of the God of all grace. God would lead them to into a settled, peaceful place of maturity and fruitfulness. We naturally focus on trials and difficulties. Perhaps we should pause and think of the effects of God's grace in His children.

God takes us through these spiritual experiences to develop us into the people He wants us to be. He places us in circumstances which are intended to increase our faith in Him and our confidence in His grace. The local expression of His Church is the place where we are established and put down roots. It is also the place where we are spiritually fed through the ministry of God's word and where we pray and enjoy fellowship. We are settled so that we can grow, mature and bear fruit, more fruit and much fruit (see John 15:2,8). Peter had walked this path with the God of all grace. It had shaped him into the peaceful, gentle, humble shepherd he had become. As he considers the grace of God in the lives of His people, his heart overflows in worship: "To Him be the glory and the dominion forever and ever. Amen" (1 Peter 5:11). So should ours!

Day 31

Tuesday

The God of all comfort

Blessed be the God and Father of our Lord Jesus Christ, the Father of mercies and God of all comfort, who comforts us in all our tribulation, that we may be able to comfort those who are in any trouble, with the comfort with which we ourselves are comforted by God.   (2 Corinthians 1:3-4)

The God and Father of our Lord Jesus Christ

Paul had to address several serious problems in his first letter to the Corinthian assembly, and they had responded to his ministry. He starts his second letter by lifting up his heart to God in worship, "Blessed be the God and Father of our Lord Jesus Christ." The Lord Jesus spoke to Mary, on the resurrection day, of ascending to "my Father and your Father, to my God and your God" (John 20:17). The Holy Spirit would always lift our hearts to praise the God and Father of our Lord Jesus: we are His children. All our blessings come because the Father sent the Lord Jesus Christ. He is the Lord of all, our Saviour, Jesus, and the One anointed to fulfil all the purposes of God, the Christ. How thankful the Apostle was that God had answered his prayers and faithfulness by blessing the saints in Corinth!

The Father of mercies

He also addresses God as "the Father of mercies". Mercy is the practical expression of the compassion we feel towards those in need. It is seen in all its fullness in God "who is rich in mercy, because of His great love with which He loved us, even when we were dead in trespasses, made us alive together with Christ (by grace you have been saved) (Ephesians 2:4-5). God displays His mercy towards us throughout our lives (Psalm 23:6).

And it is the manifold mercy of God which constantly encourages us to live sacrificial and sanctified lives:

> I beseech you therefore, brethren, by the mercies of God, that you present your bodies a living sacrifice, holy, acceptable to God, which is your reasonable service (Romans 12:1).

The God of all comfort

Comfort here means to call to one's side to encourage and help. We experience it when our parents, friends and even strangers come alongside in times of need. We also know the sense of helplessness when loved ones are so distressed that we cannot comfort them. But Paul describes God as the God of all comfort who sympathises in every situation and can meet needs others cannot.

God's power to comfort His people throughout the Old Testament was demonstrated from His throne and through His servants on earth. But the day came when God sent His Son; no longer using servants, but becoming a Servant; no longer unseen in heaven, but present in the world He had made. He came alongside the broken-hearted, the poor, the diseased, the oppressed and even the dead. While dying Himself, Jesus could say to a thief, "Today you will be with Me in Paradise" (Luke 23:43).

The Lord Jesus came alongside us in all our distance from God so that we would be forever close to Him in heaven. It is a ministry He continues now as our Great High Priest in glory. And the Holy Spirit is our Comforter on earth. May our experience of the God of all comfort make us sensitive to the needs of others and comfort them with the comfort of God.

Day 32

Watch and pray

Praying always with all prayer and supplication in the Spirit, being watchful to this end with all perseverance and supplication for all the saints. (Ephesians 6:18)

Lockdown significantly restricted what we could do, but there is one thing we can always do: pray. I have been so encouraged by recent answers to prayer. Sometimes we learn that something has happened, and we immediately recognise it as an answer to prayer and give thanks to God. At other times it takes longer to sink in!

Prayer begins with worship:

"Our Father in heaven,/Hallowed be your name."

Prayer seeks God's will:

"Your kingdom come,/Your will be done,/On earth as it is in heaven."

Prayer seeks God's provision:

"Give us this day our daily bread."

Prayer encourages forgiveness:

"And forgive us our debts,/As we forgive our debtors."

Prayer encourages holiness:

"And do not lead us not into temptation,/But deliver us from the evil one" (Matthew 6:9-13).

Paul also teaches us to pray in a spirit of thankfulness: "Be anxious for nothing, but in everything by prayer and supplication, with thanksgiving, let your requests be made known to God." Through prayer, we experience peace: "and the peace of God, which surpasses all understanding, will guard your hearts and minds through Christ Jesus (Philippians 4:6-7).

The Lord Jesus teaches so much about how to pray for others. In Luke 22:31-32 we read:

The Lord said, "Simon, Simon! Indeed, Satan has asked for you (plural), that he may sift you as wheat. But I have prayed for you (singular), that your faith should not fail; and when you have returned to Me, strengthen your brethren."

The Lord addresses Peter as Simon, indicating the natural man. He knew Satan was acting against all His disciples; this has never changed. But He prayed for Peter. The Lord Jesus prayed for his faith, his recovery and his future service. The Lord exhorts us to be "watchful". He watched over His disciples like a shepherd watching over his flock. He anticipated danger and addressed it through prayer. Like Peter, we are capable of dreadful failure. We need to be aware of Satan's schemes (Ephesians 6:11). He can act as an angel of light as well as a roaring lion. The Lord teaches us to be "watchful to this end with all perseverance and supplication for all the saints". Our prayers should be proactive as well as reactive.

As we pray for the needs of others, the Lord Jesus deepens our understanding of those needs and opens our eyes to further needs. In doing so, He brings before us the things that we can do. Yesterday we read about the God of comfort who encourages us and, in doing so, enables us to help others. Prayer isn't passive and it leads us into action. In Acts 16, when the Gospel first came to Europe, prayer is associated with the conversion of Lydia, the deliverance of the slave girl and the salvation of the Philippian jailor. Prayer is vital to everything we do, and a ministry every child of God is involved in. It takes us into God's presence, and attunes us to God's heart, mind and will. It is where we start each day.

Day 33

Another Helper

"I will pray the Father, and He will give you another Helper, that He may abide with you forever – the Spirit of truth."

(John 14:16-17)

The Holy Spirit is a Person in the Godhead, and His activity and energy are seen throughout the Bible, beginning with Creation: "And the Spirit of God was hovering over the face of the waters" (Genesis 1:2). The Spirit of God was in operation in the Old Testament in building the Tabernacle (Exodus 31:3); in writing the Scriptures (2 Timothy 3:16); in the lives of the prophets (2 Peter 1:21) and kings, like David who refers in Psalm 139:7 to the Holy Spirit's omnipresence, when he asks, "Where can I go from Your Spirit?" Whenever God acts, the Holy Spirit is working. This is especially so in the life of Christ. Of the Incarnation we read: "The Holy Spirit will come upon you, and the power of the Highest will overshadow you: therefore, also, that Holy One who is to be born will be called the Son of God" (Luke 1:35). When Jesus begins His ministry, the Holy Spirit is active "...the Holy Spirit descended in bodily form like a dove upon Him..." (Luke 3:22). When Jesus reads from Isaiah in Nazareth, He begins with the words: "The Spirit of the Lord is upon me..." (Luke 4:18).

The Holy Spirit's presence and power were not only evident throughout Christ's life, but in His sacrifice: "Christ, who through the eternal Spirit offered Himself without spot to God..." (Hebrews 9:14). The Holy Spirit is mentioned as part of the Trinity by the resurrected Christ in Matthew 28:19. At the end of Mark's Gospel, Jesus speaks of the powerful signs of the Holy Spirit. In Luke 24:49 Jesus promises to send the Holy Spirit. The coming of the Holy Spirit was the evidence of the Saviour's ascension and glory (see John 7:38-39).

The Spirit of God was active and vital at the birth of Christ's Church at Pentecost: "…you will be baptised with the Holy Spirit not many days from now" (Acts 1:5). Through the Holy Spirit's gifts and ministry in Christ's disciples the Church grows: "…but the manifestation of the Spirit is given to each one for the profit of all" (1 Corinthians 12:7). The ministry of the Holy Spirit looks forward to Christ's return. The Holy Spirit is in the first chapter of the Bible, and in its last chapter: "the Spirit and the bride say, "Come!" (Revelation 22:17). It is both humbling and uplifting to understand that this glorious Person dwells in us (see 1Corinthians 6:19-20).

The Lord Jesus humbled Himself to become our Saviour. The Holy Spirit came down to be our Helper and to continue His caring ministry. His work is to glorify Christ and to produce the fruit of the Spirit in us: to make us Christlike. He helps us in our weakness. When we don't know what to pray for, He expresses all our needs with a depth of understanding which is beyond words and comes from the very heart of God (Romans 8:26). He fills our hearts with worship and, as the Spirit of Truth, guides us through the Word of God, which is described as the "sword of the Spirit" in Ephesians 6:17. He empowers our witness (Acts 1:8).

> "I will ask the Father, and he will give you another advocate to help you and be with you forever— the Spirit of truth… you know him, for he lives with you and will be in you. I will not leave you as orphans; I will come to you" (John 14:16-18, NIV).

The Lord Jesus has not left us isolated.

Day 34

What does a living sacrifice look like?

I beseech you therefore, brethren, by the mercies of God, that you present your bodies a living sacrifice, holy, acceptable to God, which is your reasonable service. And do not be conformed to this world, but be transformed by the renewing of your mind, that you may prove what is that good and acceptable and perfect will of God. (Romans 12:1-2)

We may have read Romans 12:1 many times, but do we ever ask ourselves, "What does a living sacrifice look like?" From verse 9 onwards I think Paul answers this question by describing the spiritual features of those who would respond to his heartfelt appeal. Let's look at those features:

Genuine love – *Let love be without hypocrisy* (v. 9),

Compassion and consideration – *Be kindly affectionate to one another with brotherly love, in honour giving preference to one another* (v. 10),

Devotedness – *Not lagging in diligence, fervent in spirit, serving the Lord* (v. 11),

Joy, patience, prayerfulness – *Rejoicing in hope, patient in tribulation, continuing steadfastly in prayer* (v. 12),

Cheerful giving – *Distributing to the needs of the saints, given to hospitality* (v. 13),

Blessing – *Bless those who persecute you; bless and do not curse* (v. 14),

Sympathy – *Rejoice with those who rejoice, and weep with those who weep* (v. 15),

Harmony and humility – *Be of the same mind toward one another. Do not set your mind on high things, but associate with the humble. Do not be wise in your own opinion* (v. 16),

Integrity – *Have regard for good things in the sight of all men* (v. 17),

Gentleness – *... live peaceably with all men* (v. 18),

Overcoming – *...overcome evil with good* (vv. 19-21).

Outside the Tabernacle was a large container, full of water, called the Laver. The priests took water from the Laver to wash. It was made from bronze mirrors donated by the women of Israel (Exodus 38:8). Through its still water, the priests would have seen their reflections as they took the water to cleanse themselves. Most mornings, we look in a mirror to check our appearance. But there is another mirror we need to look into – the word of God. It looks deep into our hearts and souls and it keeps us from being conformed to this world, and transforms us, by the renewing of our minds, into the likeness of the Lord Jesus. It tells us what a living sacrifice looks like. We discover what we are, and we are empowered to become what God wants us to be.

Day 35

The wisdom from above

But the wisdom that is from above is first pure, then peaceable, gentle, willing to yield, full of mercy and good fruits, without partiality and without hypocrisy. Now the fruit of righteousness is sown in peace by those who make peace. (James 3:17-18)

James pulls no punches in laying bare the harm caused by failing to control our speech. He begins his discourse on "the tongue" in James 3:1-12 by addressing spiritual leaders. James explains that teachers of the word of God will be held to account for the consistency of their words and actions. Then he makes it clear that all Christians are responsible for what they say. James was very aware of how easy it is to say the wrong thing or to be misunderstood: "If anyone does not stumble in word, he is a perfect man, able also to bridle the whole body" (James 3:2). How many times have I had to say to myself, "I wish I hadn't said that" or "I didn't mean to say that". One of the few men in the Bible who knew how to control his tongue was Samuel; he let "none of his words fall to the ground" (1 Samuel 3:19).

James warns us that, although the tongue is small, it is capable of enormous harm. He uses the powerful illustration of how a tiny flame can start a great forest fire (James 3:5) to describe the destructive power of uncontrolled speech and the poisonous nature of slander and gossip. Particularly chastening is how James highlights the hypocrisy of singing the praises of God and employing beautiful language in prayer, then deploying language to belittle and damage fellow believers (3:9-12). Adding to this, he comments on the bitterness of envy and self-seeking and all the confusion and evil that results (3:14-16). So much damage is caused by what is said nationally and internationally in the name of religion and politics. And enormous harm is also done by what is spoken locally, in families and amongst the people of God. It is a real and present danger.

But James does not merely condemn what is wrong: he describes the wisdom which is from above as the remedy. James' description of the wisdom from above has a beautiful calmness. There are two aspects to wisdom: insight and application. God's word provides both. In verse 17 James uses a word for the character of wisdom and then outlines its application. His description starts with its purity. We live in an impure world. The wisdom from above is pure, and stimulates our holiness. It is peaceable and promotes harmony and encourages Christlike gentleness in us. Wisdom from above teaches us not to continually want our own way, but to think of others. It is full of mercy and actively seeks to meet the needs of others. This wisdom is fruitful, a sign of abiding in Christ, and the fruit of the Spirit. And it does not favour others based on position or relationship; it does not have double standards. James describes the actions of those who make peace as seed which produces the fruit of righteousness.

James ruthlessly exposes the dangers of an unruly tongue and then brings before us the calm, powerful and healing ministry of living in the light of the wisdom of God. This comes from above, and that is where we must begin to look each day.

Day 36

Sunday

Woven from the top

Then the soldiers, when they had crucified Jesus, took His garments and made four parts, to each soldier a part, and also the tunic. Now the tunic was without seam, woven from the top in one piece. (John 19:23)

And Jesus cried out again with a loud voice, and yielded up His spirit. Then, behold, the veil of the temple was torn in two from top to bottom. (Matthew 27:50-51)

I remember my wife, June, knitting a beautiful circular shawl as a present for our first grandchild, Naomi. What made it most remarkable was that it had no seam. It was knitted on a circular needle from the top to the bottom.

Interestingly, the clothes of the Lord Jesus are mentioned at the beginning and end of His life. He was wrapped in swaddling clothes and laid in a manger at His birth. This description gives us a sense of how the Eternal Son of God confined Himself within a tiny body to become our Saviour. The angels remind us of the heights from which He came and the lowliness of the manger.

John recalls the cruel indifference of the soldiers at Calvary. They shared, then drew lots for all that the Lord owned in this world – His clothes. They could, in pity, have given these to Mary, who was standing by. But, no: they took everything. John reminds us that the tunic was woven from the top to the bottom. In Mark 5:27 the woman stretched out her hand in faith to touch the Lord's garment and to be healed. These two incidents are vivid reminders of the Lord's perfect seamless life of grace in this world: who He was, woven from the top; a life sacrificed in love, woven to the bottom. These were the clothes the Lord of Glory wore as He expressed the heart of God to this world.

Matthew records the Lord's death in all its horror and pain, and what happened in the Temple when Jesus gave His life. The veil of the Temple was torn in two from the top to the bottom. As Jesus gave Himself, God acted by tearing in two the Temple curtain, exposing the Most Holy Place. We read in Hebrews 10:19-20: "Therefore, brothers and sisters, since we have confidence to enter the Most Holy Place by the blood of Jesus, by a new and living way opened for us through the curtain, that is, his body…" (NIV). The immediacy with which God responds to the death of His Son is compelling.

John writes of the empty tomb, the clothes lying, and the handkerchief folded – the work finished (John 20:5-8). John was there when Jesus raised Lazarus from the dead and told his friends to free him from his grave clothes. The Lord Jesus needed no one to loose and set Him free; He is the resurrection and the life. As the Good Shepherd, He had the power to give His life and to take it again in resurrection.

In Bethlehem, there was no room in the inn. At Calvary, everything was taken from Him. But Calvary isn't the story of what men took away: it is the story of what the Lord Jesus gave. We should never tire of tracing that journey of love and rejoicing in His glorious resurrection and how He was taken up in glory into heaven. Thomas only believed because he saw (John 20:29). We never saw Jesus walk in grace through this world, but we "know the grace of our Lord Jesus Christ, that though He was rich, yet for your sakes He became poor, that you through His poverty might become rich" (2 Corinthians 8:9). It touches the heart of the Saviour that we remember His love and worship Him.

Day 37

Aquila and Priscilla: A secure marriage

After these things Paul departed from Athens, and came to
Corinth; And found a certain Jew named Aquila, born in
Pontus, lately come from Italy, with his wife Priscilla; (because
that Claudius had commanded all Jews to depart from Rome:)
and came unto them. And because he was of the same craft, he
abode with them, and wrought: for by their occupation they were
tentmakers. (Acts 18:1-3, AV)

A young couple was invited to a diamond wedding celebration.
During the evening, the young woman had an opportunity to
speak to the elderly lady who had been married for sixty years.
She said to her, "I can't get over how long you've been married.
Sixty years is over twice my lifetime, and I've been married for
less than a year. Tell me, what do you have in common with
your husband?" The old lady thought deeply for a while, then
replied, "We were married on the same day!"

Aquila and Priscilla had a long and successful marriage and
shared so much. They are an outstanding example of Christian
marriage. We first meet them at the start of Acts 18 and
soon learn how strong their marriage was and how it proved
such a blessing to others. Today we hear a lot about marriage
breakdown. It is disturbing that more and more Christian
marriages are failing. In the Gospels, the Lord Jesus told the
parable of the wise and foolish builders. One built his house
on sand – a weak foundation! When the storm came, it
collapsed. The other builder founded his home on a rock, and
it withstood the storm. Marriage is like a building. It needs the
right foundation. Aquila and Priscilla's marriage had the right

foundation. That is why the persecution they suffered in Rome did not damage their marriage or take away the joy of their salvation. The hatred of Emperor Claudius for the Jews had cost them their home and livelihood in Rome. Yet in Corinth we find them happily re-establishing a home and their tent-making business, and inviting the Apostle Paul to live and work with them – a friendship which lasted until Paul's death.

So what were the foundations which made their marriage so robust and their care for others so outstanding? It was based upon knowing God. Whenever we think about couples getting married, we concentrate upon them knowing each other well enough to take the greatest act of faith people ever demonstrate towards each another. As Christians, before we enter such a relationship, it is vital to have a right relationship with God. Adam, the first man to get married, helps us to understand this. He had a living relationship with God. He knew God as his Creator, Friend and Guide. God gave Adam responsibility and authority in Eden. It was after he had experienced this stable relationship with God that he entered the unique relationship he had with his wife Eve. Knowing God's love and direction in his own life prepared him for his relationship with Eve. All this happened before sin entered the world.

Aquila and his wife Priscilla are characterised by their actions, not their words. The love of God stimulated these actions and was demonstrated so clearly in the love they had for each other. If the young woman above had the opportunity to ask Priscilla what she had in common with her husband Aquila, she would have learned of the love and grace of God that filled Priscilla and Aquila's hearts and marriage. It was a love that overcame their suffering, motivated their work, embraced their friends, welcomed people into their home, built up the people of God, a sacrifice from warm and tender hearts. They didn't have things in common; they were one.

Day 38

Aquila and Priscilla: A sanctified marriage

A bishop then must be blameless, the husband of one wife.

(1 Timothy 3:2)

Over time, man has changed God's model of marriage. Men often had several wives; King Solomon had 700 (1 Kings 11:3). Women were owned as property and often abused. But Christianity reaffirmed God's model: a lifelong union between one man and one woman. Paul writes in 1 Timothy 3:2, "A bishop then must be blameless, the husband of one wife." Today, this concept of marriage is considered unrealistic. Yet, when a marriage fails, people yearn for this ideal relationship and often remarry. The desire for this God-appointed relationship is still widespread.

Aquila and Priscilla's marriage was characterised by knowing God. Christians should prepare for marriage by asking for God's guidance to be led to the right person with whom you will share your life. The marriage relationship must be open and based upon genuine love and trust. It is essential to have spiritual help and guidance from spiritual and experienced Christian married couples as part of this preparation. It is crucial to approach marriage thoughtfully and carefully. And, if your marriage gets into difficulty, seek help earlier rather than later. Time is of the essence if a breakdown is taking place. A good marriage can fail, but a failing marriage can be restored.

The Lord Jesus was central to Aquila and Priscilla's marriage because He was central to their lives. This is not always the case. Their faith and daily trust in Christ gave them the resources to understand how to work things out when trouble came along. We live in a throwaway world. We use up things, then get replacements. If our television or washing machine breaks down, we change them. This is reflected in our relationships. These often only survive while things go well but, when difficulties arise, relationships can be abandoned. Even Christians can become resigned to this trend and put it down to the days we live in, ceasing to express faith in the God of reconciliation.

Aquila and Priscilla's marriage faced enormous difficulties, but God enabled them to overcome these pressures. Trouble brought them closer to God and to each other. How do we handle difficulties in our marriages? Do we endure them alone until they became unbearable? As a husband do I fail to see the physical, emotional or spiritual struggles my wife has? Or do I personally take responsibility to understand and help her in such circumstances? Equally, a husband needs the same response from his wife.

Communication is crucial to marriage. It involves explaining, listening and learning. We need to explain to each other the things which encourage us and the things which concern us. We also need to listen – not only to the words that are being said but recognising the emotions behind them. Listening is so beneficial. Think of the times when a friend simply listened to you. Afterwards, the circumstances had not changed, but you felt much better, simply because someone listened and understood. God is the best listener there is. His ear and His heart are never closed to us, and neither should ours be to each other. Make time to listen and act on what you learn. Communication is about learning. The Lord's words "Learn of Me" are vital. He wants us to learn from Him in all the experiences we pass through as man and wife. Go into God's presence together and pray for and with each other. This is the way we build and strengthen our marriages and become better able to demonstrate His love and power in them.

Day 39

Wednesday

Aquila and Priscilla: A spiritual and supportive marriage

And Paul after this tarried there yet a good while, and then took his leave of the brethren, and sailed thence into Syria, and with him Priscilla and Aquila. (Acts 18:18, AV)

Priscilla and Aquila's marriage was not a self-centred one. So many marriages break down so quickly. This often has to do with couples carrying on as single people after they are married. Time is not given to developing a happy marriage that will grow and prosper. Self-absorption is another problem. Couples can become so absorbed with each other that there is no place or time for anyone else. This approach can stifle a marriage and create problems. A healthy marriage is balanced. Priscilla and Aquila's relationship was characterised by the love of God. They were devoted to each other, but their love flowed out to others in friendship, service, and sacrifice. They were amongst Paul's closest friends and consistently supported him. We should not forget the responsibility we have to serve God together. There will always be those within and outside our families who need us. Priscilla and Aquila instinctively responded to the needs of others.

This is demonstrated in Acts 18:24-28 when Aquila and Priscilla, who had travelled with Paul to Ephesus, heard an outstanding preacher called Apollos speaking at the synagogue, which he was visiting. Although he was a remarkable communicator, he only knew about the teaching of John the Baptist. Aquila and Priscilla invited him into their home (NIV) and helped him to understand the complete revelation of God in Jesus Christ. Their teaching of Apollos resulted in great blessing.

A recurring theme in the story of Aquila and Priscilla is the home. It is the place where others can see and benefit from the love which exists between a married couple. We live in a world of broken relationships and consequently broken homes. A home is a place where love is expressed between husband and wife, parents and children, families and friends. Aquila and Priscilla's home was such a place, and the Word of God was at its centre. When I was a young Christian, I was taught that "time with God" each day was an essential part of a Christian's life and also Christian marriage. In every Christian home there should be a time when the family takes the opportunity to pray and read the Scriptures together. Preparing for each day in God's presence and reviewing it with Him at the end of the day is a good practice. Marriages and families are strengthened by this "time with God".

Aquila and Priscilla's fellowship with God empowered them to understand and communicate the Word of God effectively in grace as their friendship with Apollos showed. They used their home as a base for the spiritual blessing of others. The home and hospitality play an important role. Paul reminds Timothy of the influence of his grandmother, Lois, and his mother, Eunice (2 Timothy 1:5, 3:15). Timothy had known the Scriptures from childhood because his mother and grandmother taught him at home. We must never underestimate the importance of godly women in the spiritual development of young people and of the people of God generally. Marriage is God's basis for family life, and all the relationships it provides. The role of grandparents should be valued. Parents and grandparents should not interfere in the marriages of their children but use their knowledge, wisdom and experience to support their children and grandchildren in grace.

Day 40

Thursday

Aquila and Priscilla: A sacrificial marriage

Greet Priscilla and Aquila my helpers in Christ Jesus: Who have for my life laid down their own necks: unto whom not only I give thanks, but also all the churches of the Gentiles. Likewise greet the church that is in their house. (Romans 16:3-5, AV)

In Romans 16:3-5 we learn more about the marriage of Priscilla and Aquila. Paul explains these dear friends risked their lives for him. The neck conveys the idea of being equally yoked together and beautifully illustrates the unity of motive and action which characterised Priscilla and Aquila. Paul names lots of friends in the New Testament but never thinks of Priscilla without Aquila. These two people were never separated in the minds of those who knew them and had experienced their sacrificial love. Sacrificial love is at the basis of Christian marriage.

On our wedding day (those who choose to marry), we stand before God, our family, friends and many other witnesses to promise a lifelong faithfulness. For this promise to work, we have to be prepared for sacrifice. I have to be prepared to sacrifice my interests for those of my wife. Equally, she has to be ready to respond. It is the most beautiful and humbling human experience to know that someone loves you so much that they are prepared to sacrifice for your good. The standard is Christ Himself (see Ephesians 5:25). The love a husband has for his wife should be a reflection of Christ's love for his Church. The Ephesian church was rebuked in Revelation 2:4 for the loss of its first love for Christ. When our love for Christ diminishes, our love for others follows the same path. In Ephesians 5:28-33 husbands are given the responsibility for nourishing and cherishing their wives. Nourishing (care) emphasises what is done and cherishing (tenderness), how it is done.

Romans 16:5 refers to the church that was in Priscilla and Aquila's house. The openness of their home is a lovely example of a couple given to hospitality. I remember very well the first time I went into the home of my Bible class teacher. He and his wife were devoted to each other and to serving the Lord. The table had all sorts of savouries and cakes on it, and all the plates and cutlery looked very special. But our hostess had forgotten to give me a knife for my side plate. When she noticed her mistake, she got a knife from the drawer and passed it to me. In my ignorance of table manners and place settings, I said, "It's all right, Mrs Packer, I've already got a knife." I didn't realise you needed two! But Mrs Packer said, "Well, you can have this one as well for your cake." As a young person, it impressed me how this gracious woman did not highlight my ignorance, but simply took me as I was. Priscilla reminds me of the 'Mrs Packers' in my life who taught me so much about the gentleness and kindness I have seen in so many Christian homes and the witness which flows from them.

In 1 Corinthians 16:19 the church which is in their house is mentioned again and Paul writes, "Aquila and Priscilla greet you heartily (or warmly) in the Lord." Often the tiniest expressions convey the most significant meaning. Aquila and Priscilla were a warm-hearted couple. Their faith was a living faith proved in all the crises of married life. It was expressed in the warmth of the love they had towards each other and to others. On our travels, we often get asked by friends to especially pass on greetings and love to fellow Christians. This demonstrates a genuine desire to encourage others and to let them know they are in their thoughts and prayers. Christian marriage should have a heart-warming effect on others.

Day 41

Aquila and Priscilla: A special marriage

Greet Prisca and Aquila.   *(2 Timothy 4:19)*

In his final mention of Priscilla and Aquila in the Bible, Paul simply writes, "Greet Prisca and Aquila." These were some of the very last words Paul wrote, as he remembered this special couple who were his dearest friends, and to whom he owed so much. Paul did not have to expand upon their lives of devoted service; their names said it all. They are only mentioned six times in the New Testament. But in these references we see how much Priscilla and Aquila had learned of Christ and shown Him to others in their outstanding marriage. I am reminded of the Lord's words in Matthew 11:29-30, "Take My yoke upon you and learn from Me, for I am gentle and lowly in heart, and you will find rest for your souls. For my yoke is easy and My burden is light." Their lives were lived as one, and they are given to us as an example of Christian marriage. It was a joyous marriage, lived out in a challenging world. It was a marriage which overcame adversity and thrived by knowing and sharing the love of God.

Several years ago I spoke at a young people's conference in Germany. I talked about Aquila and Priscilla, and Christian marriage. I introduced the subject by saying that Christian marriage is vital to all Christians. It is one of the few times I can remember being heckled in such a meeting. Two young men, who were not married, asked why the subject was essential to them. I explained that God's model for society is based on marriage and that families, communities and nations emerged from it. I emphasised that marriage witnesses to the love of

Christ. Christians should uphold its value and purpose, even if we never marry, and we should make marriage, the bringing up of children and the family central themes of our prayers. I added that young Christian men and women should prepare themselves for marriage.

Two years later, at the same conference, a young brother came to me and reminded me of my talk. He thanked me for the ministry and explained he had not appreciated what I had said at the time but had come to understand its importance. He was about to be married.

In 2017 the (UK) Office for National Statistics reported that marriage rates for opposite-sex couples were the lowest on record. It reported that only 22% of all marriages in 2017 were religious ceremonies, the lowest percentage on record. In that year nearly 9 in 10 (88%) of opposite-sex couples cohabited before getting married.

I think society has yet to understand and bear the real cost of abandoning the model of marriage God established for our well-being. This rejection didn't start in the 1970s. We can trace its roots to the beginning of society and men's treatment of women. Marriage does not guarantee love and care. But God designed marriage so love could be sacrificially expressed towards each other, our children and society. God's word tells us to hold marriage in honour (Hebrews 13:4), and Paul warns us of a world in which marriage would be forbidden (1 Timothy 4:3). God has chosen us to be His witnesses in a world that is increasingly rejecting God's paths of righteousness.

Aquila and Priscilla teach us how to be such witnesses. May our marriages, by God's grace, give honour to Him, encourage each other, and be an example and blessing in a broken world.

Day 42

Saturday

Refreshers

The Lord grant mercy to the household of Onesiphorus, for he often refreshed me, and was not ashamed of my chain; but when he arrived in Rome, he sought me out very zealously and found me.
(2 Timothy 1:16-17)

As cold waters to a thirsty soul, so is good news from a far country.
(Proverbs 25:25, AV)

I remember being at the Keswick Convention in the late 1990s when one of the speakers reminded us of some sweets we used to eat as children, which were called "Refreshers" and "Smarties". He used them as an example of the behaviours of Christians. He said some Christians can be 'Smarties', always correcting us, always putting us right; others are 'Refreshers', always encouraging and caring.

Onesiphorus was definitely a "refresher" because Paul tells us he was. Paul knew what it was like to be deserted, even by those he had served so well. Onesiphorus was a friend who didn't just encourage Paul, but "often" did so. He was not ashamed to visit the imprisoned Apostle, but went to Rome to find him. Paul describes the effort this dear man put in to see Paul. He sought him "zealously". It obviously wasn't easy to work through the Roman judicial system. But Onesiphorus was not someone who gave up quickly; He found Paul. I suspect he didn't go empty-handed. The Lord Jesus searched for us until He found us (Luke 15). It is beautiful to see this determination in the hearts of His people, both in evangelism and pastoral care. We often think of Paul's unrelenting service, but he was profoundly affected and so thankful for the kindness of the Christians he once sought to destroy – Christians, like Onesiphorus, who ensured the Apostle knew he wasn't forgotten.

My mother used to let me hold young people's meetings in our house before I was married. She had not made a profession of faith, but she cheerfully entertained us, providing drinks and biscuits. Like everyone else, I took this for granted. But I remember her being touched when one young sister brought her some tea and sugar to help with the refreshments.

Paul knew the presence of the Lord in remarkable dreams, visions and revelations from heaven. But he also knew the Lord's presence in the simple, kind acts of fellow believers: friends who visited him and friends who stayed by him. During lockdown, we have appreciated the help of new technology. We are thankful to see each other on a computer screen even though we are miles apart. But not everyone has this facility and more deeply miss what it is to see each other, shake hands, embrace, greet each other with a holy kiss and talk face to face. They need a refreshing letter, a card, a telephone call, until we can freely visit again.

Over the past week, we received two letters and experienced the refreshment and joy of the words of Proverbs, "As cold waters to a thirsty soul, so is good news from a far country." We all need such refreshment, and may the Lord help us to be "refreshers".

Day 43

Always with us

I am with you always.   *(Matthew 28:20)*

It is fundamental to the Christian experience to know the Lord's presence. He left His disciples in no doubt that He would not desert them. Of course, the Lord Jesus is no longer physically here in this world. He is in heaven. But we should not think He is confined within a place. God is omnipresent – all-present. He is distinct from His creation, but present in it. Creation also witnesses to God's omnipotence. He is all-powerful. God is supreme and has power over everything seen and unseen. This power is infinite. God is also omniscient – all-knowing. His knowledge embraces the past, the present and the future; He knows all things. These characteristics of God are beyond our comprehension.

It is the most astonishing thing to realise that the Person who made and sustains all things makes His presence known to His people; we know Him personally. The atheist thinks this is nonsense. Why would an all-powerful God have a relationship with tiny insignificant creatures on one tiny insignificant planet? But why do we assume that what is tiny is insignificant? We have all seen amazing images of the wonder and immensity of the observable universe. But do these come close to the complexity and beauty of what is found in your garden, the animal kingdom, the mysteries of the oceans and the wonder of the human body, mind and spirit?

The greatness of God is not confined to the scale and wonder of His creation. It is seen in Who He is: God is light and God is love. The revelation of who God is does not lie in the stars and planets, but in the lowliness and love of Jesus Christ. It was revealed at Calvary where He died in love for this world. In this tiny location, God chose to demonstrate the vastness of His eternal love and grace.

I was speaking to some children at a Christian conference last year. I wrote out the word "Goodbye" in different languages, and we had a lot of fun reading them together. But then I told the children something which I had not considered before. I said to them that Jesus never said, "Goodbye". He told His disciples He was leaving them to go back to heaven. They were with Him the day that happened. They saw Him taken up in glory. But He never said "Goodbye" to them. He said, "I am with you always." And more than this, He promised them the Holy Spirit:

"And I will pray the Father, and He will give you another Helper, that He may abide with you forever— the Spirit of truth, whom the world cannot receive, because it neither sees Him nor knows Him; but you know Him, for He dwells with you and will be in you. I will not leave you orphans; I will come to you" (John 14:16-18).

This morning as the people of God, we experience those words, "I will come to you." He promised that "where two or three are gathered together in My name, I am there in the midst of them" (Matthew 18:20). The love of the omnipresent, omnipotent and omniscient God was revealed in Jesus of Nazareth. In the Lord's supper, we remember His love, we joy in His presence with us, and we look forward to the day when He will bring all His people to where He is. This bows our hearts in worship.

Day 44

Monday

The shoulders of the Shepherd

"What man of you, having a hundred sheep, if he loses one of them, does not leave the ninety-nine in the wilderness, and go after the one which is lost until he finds it? And when he has found it, he lays it on his shoulders, rejoicing." *(Luke 15:4-5)*

There is a service station at the northern end of the M6 motorway. In the restaurant is a large and striking photograph of an old, smiling Cumbrian shepherd with a lamb on his shoulders. It always reminds me of Luke 15. Isaiah 9:6 speaks of the Lord and the government of the world being "upon his shoulder". We often compare this to the shepherd's shoulders in Luke 15 where the Lord speaks, not of His "shoulder" of government, but of "his shoulders" of salvation. It is an illustration of the depth and power of His redeeming love. The old hymn powerfully expresses this thought:

> But none of the ransomed ever knew
> How deep were the waters crossed;
> Nor how dark was the night which the Lord passed
> through
> Ere He found His sheep that was lost. (E. C.
> Clephane)

In Luke 15 the Lord Jesus gives a beautiful picture of Himself. The shepherd searches for one lost sheep and finds it and brings it safely home. It is the story of three journeys. The journey the lost sheep took, the journey the shepherd took and the journey of the shepherd with His sheep. The first journey describes where we were without God – lost. The second journey represents the cost of our salvation – Jesus coming to where we were. And the third journey describes the joy and power of a love from which we can never be separated, and of our glorious destiny.

In John's Gospel Jesus doesn't give us an illustration; He tells us clearly, "I am the good shepherd. The good shepherd gives His life for the sheep" (John 10:11). He wanted us to understand, without any doubt, His love for us.

In Luke 23 the Lord Jesus does not speak in a parable, nor does He describe who He is; He proves it. If ever a man was lost, it was the dying thief. Jesus, in the very act of dying as the Saviour of the world, finds this man: "And Jesus said to him, 'Assuredly, I say to you, today you will be with Me in Paradise'" (v. 43).

The Lord's shepherd-heart continues to be seen in His resurrection. He finds Mary, the two on the road to Emmaus, Thomas and Peter. He went to where they were in their sorrow and confusion, and in their unbelief and failure. He drew them to Himself. He showed them the wounds of the Good Shepherd. He assured them that His ministry of grace and love would continue to sustain and empower them. The Lord makes Mary His messenger; sets alight the hearts of the two disciples on the road to Emmaus; makes Thomas a worshipper, and Peter a shepherd.

The Lord's shepherd's-heart has not changed. Let's rest in Him, worship Him, follow Him, witness to Him and never forget that His love will carry us home.

Day 45

The searching of the Spirit

"Or what woman, having ten silver coins, if she loses one coin, does not light a lamp, sweep the house, and search carefully until she finds it? And when she has found it, she calls her friends and neighbours together, saying, 'Rejoice with me, for I have found the piece which I lost!' Likewise, I say to you, there is joy in the presence of the angels of God over one sinner who repents."

(Luke 15:8-10)

In the three parables Jesus uses in Luke 15 He gives us an insight into the heart of God displayed through God the Son, God the Spirit and God the Father. Yesterday we thought of Jesus represented as the shepherd. Today we see the searching work of the Holy Spirit in the parable of lost silver coin.

The Lord Jesus, in telling these stories, was reaching out to two audiences: those who had bad reputations, the tax collectors and sinners, and those who were self-righteous, the Pharisees and scribes. He uses language and settings both audiences understood, and they would relate to the importance of a valuable lost coin. But the Lord doesn't present the lost silver coin in isolation. It was part of a treasured set of ten silver coins.

The shepherd is an illustration of the Person and work of the Lord Jesus. It displays His redeeming love towards each of us. The woman is an illustration of the Person and work of the Holy Spirit. His work is to glorify the Lord Jesus, and a vital part of this is bringing people to salvation.

The first thing the woman did was to light a lamp. In Psalm 119:105, the word of God is described as "a lamp for my feet, a light on my path" (NIV). In John, the Holy Spirit is called "the Spirit of Truth" (John 14:17). We read of the "sword of the Spirit, which is the word of God" in Ephesians 6:16. The Spirit of God uses the word of God to convict people of their need of the Saviour and to bring them to salvation. The Lord also describes the woman sweeping the house. Rather like the sower, there is an expansiveness about the work of the Spirit. At the same time, there is a focus on the individual. The woman searched carefully until she found the lost coin. Here the language is the same as in the story of the lost sheep where the shepherd searched until he found the lost sheep.

Both parables end in joy. In Hebrews 12: 2 speaks of Jesus as "the author and finisher of *our* faith, who for the joy that was set before Him endured the cross, despising the shame, and has sat down at the right hand of the throne of God".

The Holy Spirit has ministered ceaselessly through the day of grace to bring people to Christ. He works through the people of God and the word of God to bring the light of the Gospel into this dark world and embrace the redeemed within the body of Christ. And He connects us with the joy of heaven by filling our hearts with joy in the Holy Spirit (Rom 14:17). It is a work that should always be upon our hearts.

Day 46

The Father's heart

"But the father said to his servants, 'Bring out the best robe and put it on him, and put a ring on his hand and sandals on his feet. And bring the fatted calf here and kill it, and let us eat and be merry; for this my son was dead and is alive again; he was lost and is found.' And they began to be merry." (Luke 15:22-24)

In the final parable in Luke 15 the Lord Jesus gives us a beautiful insight into the heart of God. But the story begins with what was in the heart of the youngest son: "Father, give me..." These three words describe so clearly how the youngest son saw his father – only as a giver. It is a telling picture of people's view of God. They want God to give them exactly what they want and not to interfere in their lives. I cannot recall how many times people have said to me, "If there is a God, why doesn't He... ?" The extraordinary feature of this story is that the father gave his son everything he requested. And the first thing he did was to leave.

We believe we can do so much better by ourselves, despite the overwhelming evidence to the contrary. The youngest son illustrates the consequences of putting a great distance between himself and the father who loved him. He didn't lose everything: he spent everything. No one took his inheritance away: he gave it away. He was responsible for his loss. And when he had nothing, he learned the bitter lesson that the world would give him nothing. But it was the loss of everything which transformed his life. I remember a brother telling me how he grew up in a Christian home and turned his back on the faith of his parents. He woke one night, in the gutter, after another bout of heavy drinking, and in the words of Luke 15 "he came to himself."

The son never understood his father's heart whilst he lived at home. It was when he returned home in rags and repentance that he experienced the profound love his father had for him. The father had longed for his son's return and the speed with which the father ran to his son was far greater than the speed at which the son approached his father. The son was overwhelmed by a sense of unworthiness. But the father never allowed him to say the words, "Make me like one of you hired servants." The son only wanted to be safe; he had no expectation of the love that overwhelmed him. But he didn't enter the father's house as a servant. He entered as a beloved son, clothed, not in rags, but in the best robe; not in poverty but with a ring on his finger; and not in shame, but with shoes on his feet. The son discovered how great a giver his father was, and he understood, for the first time, the source of that giving: a love which dealt with his need and sin and transformed him by its power. It is an amazing picture of God's love for us.

Why did the publicans and sinners draw near to Jesus at the beginning of Luke 15? They knew in their hearts the emptiness, not of what they had lost, but what they had accumulated. As with Zacchaeus, they had been drawn by that emptiness to the Saviour, never realising the Saviour had come to meet them. They, like so many, including ourselves, knew a time when they did not understand the immensity of the steps that God the Son, God the Holy Spirit and God the Father took to redeem us and transform us into the children of God. The Father has clothed us in the righteousness of Christ, He has sealed us with the Holy Spirit, and He has caused us to walk as His children. Surprisingly, it is possible to forget how deeply I am loved by God. At such times, we can thank the prodigal son for reminding us of the Father's heart. It is a discovery we should share.

Day 47

Thursday

A brother's heart

"And he said to him, 'Son, you are always with me, and all that I have is yours. It was right that we should make merry and be glad, for your brother was dead and is alive again, and was lost and is found.'"

(Luke 15:31-32)

In Luke 15:2 the Pharisees and the scribes were unhappy that the Lord Jesus reached out to the tax collectors and sinners to bring them into God's blessing. They consistently viewed the failure of others as a background from which to reflect their own righteousness (Luke 18:11). The three parables of Luke 15 teach us about the heart of God and the joy the Godhead has in the salvation of the lost. The first two parables are about the value God places on us and the action He takes to redeem us. The final parable teaches us about our rejection of God, and its consequences. We learn about turning to God in repentance. We also learn that redemption is about mercy and grace: we are not merely saved, but we become the children of God.

But the story of the prodigal son includes the story of an older brother, who never left his father's house or wasted what the father gave him. But like his younger brother he never understood his father's heart. He gives us a vivid insight into the dangers of self-righteousness. It is self-obsessed and self-glorifying. Its energy comes from our view of what we think we are, what we do, and our condemnation of failure in others. But it distances us from God and blinds us to our need of His salvation. We also make the mistake of thinking it is a religious problem, but its influence is clearly evident throughout the whole of society and it is at the root of many of the world problems. It seeks to control others, and makes people joyless and resentful of the joy others experience.

We see this in the older brother. He did not run into the room to embrace his brother. There were no kisses or tears; there was just anger, bitterness, resentment and separation. The father had to go out once more, this time to plead with his older son. It must have caused the father heartache to hear his eldest son's words: "I have served you..."; "I never transgressed..."; "You never gave me..." These were not aimed at his brother, who he discarded as an immoral man, but at his own father. Despite all the years he had spent in his father's company, he had no sense of his father's love for him.

That love was expressed in the gentle words which followed: "Son, you are always with me, and all that I have is yours." Christ loved the tax collectors, like Zacchaeus, and He also loved the Pharisees, like Saul of Tarsus. God cuts through all our need, whatever form it takes, in order to reveal His love for us. The father added, "Your brother was dead and is alive again, and was lost and is found." God's love not only deals with our distance from Him, it deals with our distance from each other. In brings us into a fellowship of life where, whatever our background, we are one in Christ Jesus. We are loved, and empowered to love each other. The elder brother resented the father who loved him and despised the brother who needed his father's love. The father added, "It was right that we should make merry and be glad." That day, mercy and truth had met together and righteousness and peace had kissed (Psalm 85:10). Self-righteousness had no place in the father's house. The Lord Jesus was challenging the hearts of the Pharisees and scribes, and He challenges ours. We are capable of building walls of separation and of destroying fellowship. God has put the best robe on us – the righteousness of Christ. It is for us to live in its dignity with our hearts full of mercy, truth and peace.

Day 48

No one ever prayed for me

Therefore He is also able to save to the uttermost those who come to God through Him, since He always lives to make intercession for them. (*Hebrews 7:25*)

George Müller was a remarkable man of faith. The orphanages he established were sustained and flourished on the basis of a simple trust in God and a belief that God would answer prayer. After his conversion he made it his business to pray for the salvation of ten of his friends. Throughout his life, these friends came, one by one, to trust in Christ. At the end of his life, George Müller was still praying for the last two of these friends. Just before his death, one more opened his heart to the Saviour. The final friend was converted shortly after his death. Müller had prayed for them for forty years!

It has always impressed me that this man of God, amid all the responsibility he had for a considerable and demanding ministry, never forgot to pray for his friends. He took upon himself the obligation to pray for their salvation.

A Christian friend of mine used to visit his local market every week. He got talking to one of the stallholders and asked him how his business was doing. The man told him his business was failing, and sadly he was going to close it. My friend asked the man if he would like him to pray for him. To his surprise, the man agreed – and the brother simply committed him to the Lord. Afterwards, the man said to him, "No one has prayed for me before." It made me wonder how many people would say the same thing.

We see in the Lord's ministry a love which reached out to all people in all circumstances. It was a focussed love. Sometimes He drew people to Himself, like Nicodemus (John 3). At other times He went to places to find people, like the woman at Sychar's well (John 4). He looked over vast crowds, and in compassion saw them as sheep not having a shepherd. But he knew and held in his heart every single person in those large companies.

I have told the story many times of a visit to a friend's farm. He took me one morning into a huge barn. Inside were well over a hundred sheep. I stood beside my friend as he looked over his flock. Then he began to walk through the sheep and took hold of one of them and gave it an injection before letting it rejoin his friends. To me, all the sheep were the same. But my friend, a shepherd, knew every sheep in his flock, and was able to address the needs of each one. That morning I learned about the character and ability of a shepherd.

Jesus Christ also teaches us about the shepherd finding the lost sheep – the work of evangelism. Sometimes, the Gospel is communicated publicly, like Phillip did in Samaria, or personally, as he did with the Ethiopian eunuch (Acts 8). We can feel inadequate in this work. But prayer is one ministry we can all undertake, especially for people we know. Throughout COVID we had the opportunity to get to know our neighbours a lot better. These are people close to us; people we can pray for and people who might say, "No one has prayed for me before." The Lord's ministry in glory is a ministry of intercession. The Holy Spirit's ministry on earth is one of intercession. It is one we can share by interceding for people in prayer. Today is a good day to make a list of friends and neighbours and to commit ourselves to bringing them to the throne of grace. We can ask, in faith, for the Lord Jesus to give us opportunities to share our faith in Him and to move in their hearts to lead them to Himself.

Day 49

Saturday

The Lord of peace

Now may the Lord of peace himself give you peace always in every way. The Lord be with you all. (2 Thessalonians 3:16)

The Lord Jesus is described as "the Lord of peace". It is through Him that we have peace with God, and have come to know the God of peace. In describing the Lord Jesus as the Lord of peace, Paul was explaining that the Saviour is able to bring peace to our hearts in every circumstance: "The Lord of peace Himself give you peace always in every way." And this is known by His presence:"The Lord be with you all."

Paul was writing from his experience. The Lord had told Ananias that He had chosen Paul to be a special witness to Him, and that as part of this witness he would suffer many things (Acts 9:15-16). Paul later records the extent of these sufferings (see 2 Corinthians 11:22-33). But his writings also convey the peace that filled his heart as he fulfilled this ministry. The secret of this peace was the Lord's abiding presence with him.

In his persecution of the Church, Paul's heart was filled with self-righteousness and rage against the Lord's people. Paul belonged to the tribe of Benjamin. Jacob, in the blessing of his sons, said of Benjamin, his youngest son, "Benjamin is a ravenous wolf" (Genesis 49:27). This violence was seen, in an extreme form, in Saul of Tarsus. The love, mercy and grace of Jesus transformed Saul, the wolf, into Paul, the shepherd. The rage he experienced was replaced by a peace which Paul himself describes as "surpassing all understanding" (Philippians 4:7). It is this peace that the Apostle wanted us to know.

Enjoying peace in our hearts does not come from being in peaceful circumstances; it comes from a Person, the Lord of Peace. And it is experienced through His presence. The Lord Jesus is always with us. We have peace with God, based on our eternally secure salvation which cannot be taken away. But that doesn't mean doubts, fear and anxiety can't fill our hearts. Such things rob us of peace. To know "peace always and in every way" comes from knowing the presence of the "Lord of peace Himself" day by day.

When I have been ill, I have always found it easy to place myself in the care of doctors. I have never had a problem being able to explain how I feel and listen to my doctor's advice, or submit to a procedure or an operation. I have confidence in the skills of those who are able to deal with ill health. But I also know many people who don't share my experience! However, I do have to ask myself if I always come with confidence and complete trust to the Saviour. Do I seek His presence, explain my feelings, and cast my care upon the Lord of peace and leave it there? Or do I endure anxiety and press on regardless, carrying the care which weighs me down? The Lord Jesus wants us to be faithful and sacrificing, but He doesn't want us to be alone, isolated in such circumstances. He wants us to develop communion with Himself and to "give us peace in every way".

Each new day is best started in the presence of the Lord of Peace: worshipping, abiding, confiding and trusting Him in the daily journeys we take.

Day 50

Sunday

Every knee shall bow

And being found in appearance as a man, He humbled Himself and became obedient to the point of death, even the death of the cross. Therefore God also has highly exalted Him and given Him the name which is above every name, that at the name of Jesus every knee should bow, of those in heaven, and of those on earth, and of those under the earth, and that every tongue should confess that Jesus Christ is Lord, to the glory of God the Father.

(Philippians 2:8-11)

I remember hearing the story of the death of one of our kings. His family were all present. When the king died, it was announced, "The king is dead, long live the king." His son, who stood by the bedside of his father, was now the king. His mother approached him, took his hand and began to kneel. Her son was embarrassed and tried to prevent his mother kneeling. But she said to him, "I want to be the first person in the kingdom to kneel before my king."

Before Paul speaks of the whole of creation *bowing down* to own Jesus as Lord, he speaks of Jesus *coming down*. He came down from heaven to make Himself of no reputation: "Is not this the carpenter's son?" (Matthew 13:55). He came down to take the form of a bondservant, as in John 13:5 "to wash the disciples' feet". He came down to become a man, as in John 4:6 "being wearied from His journey, sat thus by the well". He came down to Calvary: 'He said, "It is finished!" And bowing His head, He gave up His spirit" (John 19:30). And He came down to glorify the Father: "Father, 'into Your hands I commit My spirit'" (Luke 23:46).

The soldiers knelt before the Lord in mockery (Matthew 27:29). No one bowed down at Calvary. The world does not bow to Christ and, even within Christendom, the Lord is not universally given the first place; thereby His person and work are diminished. People choose to bow to politics, power, materialism, religion, sport and entertainment. These are the things which rule in their lives.

We come into the Lord's presence to bow before the Saviour, the Servant, the Shepherd, the Suffering Lamb, and the Son of God. His love reigns in our hearts and lifts our eyes by faith to see Him enthroned in heaven. We are in fellowship with heaven, which already enthrones the Lord Jesus Christ.

We bow in worship to the suffering Saviour who died for us, and we bow in worship to the glorified Saviour who lives for us. And in doing so we anticipate His return: "For as often as you eat this bread and drink this cup, you proclaim the Lord's death till He comes" (1 Corinthians 11:26). God has already highly exalted His Son. Our Lord and Saviour already has the name which is above every name: "Jesus".

The future is not about choice; it is about the creation-wide revelation and recognition of who Jesus is. Today we are given the unique opportunity to bow the knee now and to confess that Jesus Christ is Lord, to the glory of God the Father.

Day 51

Nehemiah, the prayers of the broken-hearted

So it was, when I heard these words, that I sat down and wept, and mourned for many days; I was fasting and praying before the God of heaven.
(Nehemiah 1:4)

Nehemiah had a good life in Persia. He had a very important job and he was highly valued by King Artaxerxes. Nehemiah was a spiritual man with a deep love for his people and the land God had given them. When his brethren from Judah visited him and told him about the destruction of the walls of Jerusalem, it broke his heart. It was a moment which changed his life and drove him into the presence of God.

Nehemiah could have sorrowed over the bitter circumstances and simply accepted that God was judging His people, who had turned their backs on Him. He could have convinced himself that conditions in Jerusalem were beyond his control, and that God had spared him to enjoy a new life with new responsibilities. But Nehemiah didn't do that. Instead, he wept, mourned, fasted and prayed. His tears were an expression of what was felt in his heart. His mourning showed the regret and sadness he experienced because of the failure of God's people. He fasted to sacrifice his own interests so as to come humbly before his God. And he prayed, recognising that only God could change the circumstances which overwhelmed him.

The Psalms tell us:

> The righteous cry out, and the LORD hears,
> And delivers them out of all their troubles.
> The Lord is near to those who have a broken heart,

And saves such as have a contrite spirit
(Psalm 34:17-18).

And Isaiah writes:

> For thus says the High and Lofty One
> Who inhabits eternity, whose name is Holy:
> "I dwell in the high and holy place,
> With him who has a contrite and humble spirit,
> To revive the spirit of the humble,
> And to revive the heart of the contrite ones
> (Isaiah 57:15).

It was from this position that Nehemiah prayed in faith. He began by worshipping God in the wonder of His Person and the power of His promises. Nehemiah simply asks God to hear his prayer. He approaches God, not only to confess the sin of his people but to associate himself in that sin. This was not an empty sentiment, but something felt deeply in his heart. He speaks to God based on His word and reverently reminds God of what He had promised. Finally, he sacrificially asks God to use him to fulfil His purposes, and places himself in the hands of God (vv. 5-11).

Nehemiah has much to teach us. He woke up to needs he could have chosen to ignore. Nehemiah was a man of compassion and spiritual insight. He felt the needs of others in his own heart, a Christlike feature. Nehemiah knew how to come into the presence of God. He teaches us about the power of a broken heart and how to touch the throne of God. Nehemiah didn't rest in his high office but placed himself humbly on the altar of God's will in complete confidence and trust.

There are many things which break our hearts, but there is only one Person who can heal them.

Day 52

Nehemiah, the prayers of the broken-hearted answered

So I became dreadfully afraid, and said to the king, "May the king live forever! Why should my face not be sad, when the city, the place of my fathers' tombs, lies waste, and its gates are burned with fire?" Then the king said to me, "What do you request?" So I prayed to the God of heaven. And I said to the king, "If it pleases the king, and if your servant has found favour in your sight, I ask that you send me to Judah, to the city of my fathers' tombs, that I may rebuild it."

(Nehemiah 2:2-5)

When Hannah had finished praying for Samuel, it says, "and her face was no longer sad" (1 Samuel 1:18). After Nehemiah had prayed to God, he continued to be sad. God had answered Hannah's prayer and healed her broken heart. Nehemiah's heart was still broken, and God used it to great effect. He wasn't only going to heal Nehemiah's broken heart, but a broken nation as well. Blessing always begins in the heart of God. He moves us into circumstances in which we begin to understand His heart and enter into His blessings.

It was a dangerous thing to be sad in the presence of kings in the days in which Nehemiah lived. He was the king's cupbearer. His role was the safety of the king, and not to be distracted with other matters. But through the grace of God, Daniel, Shadrach, Meshach, Abed-Nego, Esther and Nehemiah were not only promoted into the highest positions, but they were deeply valued and loved by those they served. The grace that kept them was manifest in them. There was an attractiveness about their godliness.

Nehemiah was both afraid and courageous. Mark Twain wisely said, "Courage is resistance to fear, mastery of fear – not absence of fear." Nehemiah may have been dreadfully afraid, but he didn't sound frightened; rather, he courteously and boldly explained his sorrow of heart. What is so amazing about the stories of Nehemiah, and other significant spiritual figures who emerged during exile, was how God moved in their lives. His timing was perfect. He placed them just where they would have the most significant effect. His used their suffering and broken heartedness to open the windows of heaven in blessing. The king did not dismiss his servant Nehemiah, but asked what he wanted. We often forget how God does not only work in *our* hearts, but He is also able to work in the hearts of those who are not His people. This should give us enormous encouragement. When we witness to the Lord, we are not by ourselves. He is with us. The Spirit of God moves people to do God's will and also to open their hearts to His salvation. We may feel fearful, but we are not alone when we witness to our Saviour, and God can surprise us by the response we get to our faithfulness.

Nehemiah teaches us to spontaneously pray to God and immediately speak to men. And he also teaches us to ask for big things; to 'rebuild a city'. It is incredible to learn that during the exile, with their freedom lost, their land taken away and their temple destroyed, the faith of men like Nehemiah and women like Esther shone so brightly. God does not want us to be cowed by the world we live in; He wants us to overcome it and to be His witnesses: "This is the victory that has overcome the world—our faith."

Day 53

Wednesday

Nehemiah, infectious faith

Then I said to them, "You see the distress that we are in, how Jerusalem lies waste, and its gates are burned with fire. Come and let us build the wall of Jerusalem, that we may no longer be a reproach." And I told them of the hand of my God which had been good upon me, and also of the king's words that he had spoken to me. So they said, "Let us rise up and build." Then they set their hands to this good work. (Nehemiah 2:17-18)

So often God works in the heart of one person, but in doing so, he ignites the hearts of many. When my daughter, Anna, was very young, I sometimes used to read her Aesop's Fables. One of these was about a cat that was very effective at catching mice. The mice had a long discussion about how to deal with the cat. In the end, one mouse proposed placing a bell around the neck of the cat so they would know when he approached, and they could hide. All the mice thought this was a brilliant idea. But then one of the mice asked who would put the bell around the cat's neck. Everyone fell silent. The plan was never carried out, and all the mice eventually died.

Nehemiah was not a mouse. He was a man of courageous faith. The task before him did not daunt him. He began his conversation with King Artaxerxes with fear in his heart, but that is not how it ended. He asked the king for everything he needed: the time, the authority and all the resources. In Daniel 1:9, God brought Daniel into the favour and goodwill of the chief of the eunuchs. In today's passage, King Artaxerxes and his queen were anxious to know how long Nehemiah would be away. It is clear to see how this man who served so well in his faithfulness to God endeared himself to the monarch. Never let us underestimate the value of living out Christ in our professions, however mundane they may seem.

I wonder what Nehemiah felt when he saw his beloved Jerusalem in ruins. I suspect he wept over the city as the Lord would do, many years later. But he was a man of vision, and I also suspect he saw in his mind and heart a city rebuilt to the glory of God and the blessing of His people. Nehemiah doesn't rush to tell the good news to his people. He waits. Nehemiah first absorbs the extent of the destruction of the walls. He had heard about it from his brethren, but now he saw the appalling damage for himself. Faith does not underestimate the challenges it faces. It counts the costs and then sets to work.

Only after surveying at night the ruins of the walls of Jerusalem does Nehemiah speak with the people. He starts at the beginning: "You see the distress that we are in, how Jerusalem lies waste, and its gates are burned with fire." Then he lifts their hearts: "Come and let us build the wall of Jerusalem, that we may no longer be a reproach." He tells them of the hand of God which had been good upon him, and also of what the king had said to him. Nehemiah's faith was infectious. The people immediately responded to his appeal: "Let us rise up and build". And so the work began.

It only needed one heart to respond in courageous faith to God. Our weakness is never an obstacle to God's power; it is the means by which it is manifested. Nehemiah's faith was recorded for our learning. "For whatever things were written before were written for our learning, that we through the patience and comfort of the Scriptures might have hope" (Romans 15:4).

Day 54

Nehemiah, building in harmony

The God of heaven Himself will prosper us; therefore we His servants will arise and build ... then Eliashib the high priest rose up with his brethren the priests and built the Sheep Gate; they consecrated it and hung its doors. (Nehemiah 2:20-3:1)

Nehemiah 3 might at first glance seem a straightforward record of how the walls and gates of Jerusalem were rebuilt. But it tells us so much about the way the people of God did the work of God. There are many helpful illustrations in this remarkable passage. I want to concentrate on the features that characterised the way the people of God worked in harmony for the glory of God.

It is very striking that the first person mentioned was Eliashib, the High Priest. It must have been a great example and a tremendous encouragement for the people to see their High Priest and his fellow priests building the Sheep Gate. They might have expected him to lead the prayers and worship which, of course, they would have done, but they worked hard just like everyone else. Alongside their brethren they cleared rubbish, laid foundations, repaired and rebuilt walls and gates. They approached their practical work in the same way as they did their spiritual responsibilities. They were an example: "nor as being lords over those entrusted to you, but being examples to the flock" (1 Peter 5:3). The spiritual shepherds built the sheep gate!

We are gradually introduced to the people who built the walls. Their names are precious to God. It is sad to learn that, although the Tekoites worked hard, the same could not be said of their nobles, who didn't put their shoulders to the work of God (v. 5). But this attitude was unusual, and it didn't stop the work. We should never let those who do not want to be committed to the work of the Lord hold back its progress. Amongst the builders were goldsmiths, perfumers, merchants, Levites and priests, who all made repairs and fortified Jerusalem. Men who were exceptional and skilled craftsmen didn't shrink from doing work so very different from their usual occupations. The leaders of the people worked alongside those they ruled over. One of them, Shallum, leader of half the district of Jerusalem, worked with his daughters on the building work (v. 12). Interestingly the Tekoites showed the devotion their nobles lacked by also repairing a further section of the wall (v. 27).

Each group worked alongside the next. Each part of the wall was linked to the next. To do this work properly required understanding, singleness of purpose, harmony, and tremendous effort and skilfulness. The workers needed a willingness to recognise the gift and ability each had, and also their limitations. They had to be willing to learn: priests would learn from craftsmen; the rich would learn from the poor; ordinary workers would benefit from working alongside their leaders and priests. And I suspect it would have been the most joyful service they had ever participated in. They would have learned so much about each other and from each other. They were not only building the walls and gates of Jerusalem; they were building a fellowship.

The building began and ended at the Sheep Gate (vv. 1, 32). It is hard not to be reminded of the Lord's words, "I am the door. If anyone enters by Me, he will be saved, and will go in and out and find pasture" and "I am the good shepherd. The good shepherd gives His life for the sheep" (John 10: 9,11). Everything begins and ends with the Lord. His love is the motivation for our worship and service.

Day 55

Friday

Nehemiah, facing opposition

So we built the wall, and the entire wall was joined together up to half its height, for the people had a mind to work.

(Nehemiah 4:6)

Opposition to the work of God often starts quietly. We are introduced to Sanballat, Tobiah and Gesham at the end of chapter 2. Things change as the work progresses, and chapter 4 records their fury, indignation and mockery. The place to deal with such opposition is in the presence of God. Nehemiah asks for God's protection as he carries on with the reconstruction of the walls of Jerusalem (vv. 4-6).

The progress was evident. The entire wall was joined together up to half its height and "the people had a mind to work". The people had a single purpose and were committed to working together. It is relatively easy to work in isolation, but God wants us to work in fellowship. We can often see service as a personal thing and take complete ownership and control of it to the exclusion of others. I love the example of Barnabas in Acts 11 when the apostles sent him to Antioch to help the new church. He was a great blessing to the people of God. But what does he do? He finds Paul and includes him in the ministry at Antioch, knowing his friend would be such a help in building up the saints in Antioch. It was the beginning of a fruitful partnership. It is a great thing to see value in our brothers and sisters and to recognise their gifts and abilities and to work side by side.

As the work grew, so did the opposition, and a surprise attack against Jerusalem was planned. Nehemiah is characterised by two vital spiritual attributes: His complete trust in God and his spiritual foresight. He knew what God could do, and he knew what he had to do. We often get confused by these two things. We can claim to trust God and be irresponsible in our actions. We can also be so determined in our efforts that we leave God out and become wilful. Nehemiah teaches us about spiritual balance: trusting and obeying. Trust is about committing our circumstances to God. Obedience is about doing God's will in those circumstances. God can work independently of us, but He also works through our obedience and actions. Nehemiah prayed for God's protection and prepared for potential danger. God answered his prayer by sending brethren to warn him of the opposition they faced. This shows us how God also moves in the hearts of our fellow brethren to support us in times of need. Nehemiah responds by preparing his workers for battle and encouraging them to trust in the Lord and to act to protect their families.

The protection of our families is paramount today. I don't think marriage in general and Christian marriages in particular have ever been in greater danger. We are involved in a spiritual battle and need to be prepared for it. We do this by trusting God, living our lives as He has directed, displaying love and care in all our family relationships, and being watchful of present dangers. Nehemiah's spiritual advice is timeless;

"Do not be afraid of them. Remember the Lord, great and awesome, and fight for your brethren, your sons, your daughters, your wives, and your houses" (4:14).

Day 56

Workers and warriors

Those who built on the wall, and those who carried burdens, loaded themselves so that with one hand they worked at construction, and with the other held a weapon. Every one of the builders had his sword girded at his side as he built.

(Nehemiah 4:17-18)

Nehemiah gives us a vivid picture of two critical aspects of the Christian life: being workers and being warriors.

Work was introduced at the beginning of creation: "Then the Lord God took the man and put him in the garden of Eden to tend and keep it" (Genesis 2:15). I remember having a conversation with our Director of Public Health. He told me how having a job benefits people suffering from mental health problems. We were created to be occupied. But work is not merely activity; it is productive and has a purpose in view. Interestingly, our first occupation, gardening, was about growing and fruitfulness. It involved Adam's body, mind and spirit. He had to work physically, he had to think about and plan his work, and it was done for the glory of God who placed him in the garden. Our work takes on a different dimension when we understand that God has placed us in it. This was the great understanding the men and women of the Exile had. They did not bemoan their plight; they accepted the circumstances God had placed them in, and they served Him there. Their spiritual lives were woven seamlessly into their work. And in that work they glorified God.

God's people were also warriors. Nehemiah instructed the people to work whilst having swords in their hands. They were ready to defend themselves. Again, this was also true in a spiritual way of the faithful people who were exiled in Babylon. They suffered the loss of their land, their beloved Jerusalem, the House of God and their freedom. But this did not diminish their faith; they were warriors. They stood, by faith, to defend their faith against the most powerful monarchs in the world. They were not reckless, proud or arrogant. Their faith was displayed in simplicity and humility, and the sword they held in their hearts was the word of God: "For the word of God is living and powerful" (Hebrews 4:12).

God has called us to be workers and warriors. As workers, we are to be "steadfast, immovable, always abounding in the work of the Lord," knowing that our labour is not in vain in the Lord (see 1 Corinthians 15:58). As warriors we are to: in our hearts "honour Christ the Lord as holy, always being prepared to make a defence" to anyone who asks us for a reason for the hope that is in us, "yet do it with gentleness and respect" (see 1 Peter 3:15 ESV).

God defeated the enemies surrounding Jerusalem without any violence taking place. But Nehemiah took nothing for granted. He knew God would protect His people, and in a hostile environment he ensured the people were prepared. Today we are called to serve God in our personal lives, relationships, marriages, families, fellowship and communities. We are also called to "fight the good fight of faith" (1 Timothy 6:12) in a world which is hostile to our faith in Jesus Christ. This encourages us to look "unto Jesus, the author and finisher of our faith, who for the joy that was set before Him endured the cross, despising the shame, and has sat down at the right hand of the throne of God" (Hebrews 12:2).

Day 57

Knowing, serving, worshipping and following the Saviour

"I am with you always, even to the end of the age." Amen.

(Matthew 28:20)

I was struck recently with the final impressions the Gospel writers leave with us. Matthew closes His Gospel with the thought of fellowship with the Lord. He records the words of Jesus: "I am with you always, even to the end of the age." Amen. The initiative to have fellowship comes from the Lord Himself. He left the world to return to heaven, but He assured His disciples of His abiding presence. This was obviously different from what they had known during the period of His ministry, in John's words: "That which was from the beginning, which we have heard, which we have seen with our eyes, which we have looked upon, and our hands have handled, concerning the Word of life". In Matthew, Jesus was talking of His spiritual presence known through the Holy Spirit, who is with us and in us. He is our link with Christ in glory. He moves our hearts to enjoy, by faith, communion with our risen Saviour and to respond to Him through His word in prayer and worship, and our faithfulness as individuals and as the people of God.

Mark ends His Gospel differently. He records the Saviour being taken up into heaven and sitting down at the right hand of God. Mark writes of Jesus as the Servant of God. It is beautiful to think of the Lord sitting down. He finished the work the Father gave Him to do. It was an eternal work that secured our eternal salvation. But he doesn't stop there; he goes on to tell us about the disciples preaching the Gospel everywhere. Then he adds, "the Lord working with them" (16:20). He presents the glorified Christ as working with His people as they witness to Him in the Gospel.

Luke records the Lord blessing His disciples and being carried up into heaven. Then he writes of them worshipping the Lord: "And they worshipped Him, and returned to Jerusalem with great joy, and were continually in the temple praising and blessing God. Amen" (24:52-53). The hearts of the glorified Lord's redeemed people are filled with joyous worship.

John starts his Gospel with the eternal glory of the Person of the Lord Jesus. At the close of his Gospel he leaves us with the simple yet vital exhortation of that same glorious Person: "Peter, seeing him, said to Jesus, "But Lord, what about this man (John)?" Jesus said to him, "If I will that he remain till I come, what is that to you? You follow Me" (21:21-22). The resurrected Saviour's desire is that every one of his disciples should live close to Him and become like Him.

In these ways, we are encouraged to live in fellowship with the Lord in communion, service, worship and discipleship. And Luke adds to these words in the first chapter of the book of Acts, as the disciples gazed up into heaven and the angels asked them, "Men of Galilee, why do you stand gazing up into heaven? *This same Jesus, who was taken up from you into heaven, will so come in like manner as you saw Him go into heaven." (Acts 1:11).* The angels assured them further that their glorious, living Saviour would return. We hasten that day in our hearts every time we break bread. We recall Jesus as the Messiah-King, the Servant of God, the Son of Man and the Son of God. As we do, He confirms His presence with us in order to remember and worship Him, and He sends us out to serve and follow Him in the sure and certain knowledge of His return. And in it all, He says, "I am with you always."

Day 58

Always abounding

Therefore, my beloved brethren, be steadfast, immovable, always abounding in the work of the Lord, knowing that your labour is not in vain in the Lord. *(1 Corinthians 15:58)*

1 Corinthians 15 is all about the glorious resurrection of Jesus Christ and the blessings emerging from it. The whole of Paul's ministry is founded on the resurrected and glorified Saviour. In Philippians 3:10-11 Paul writes, "that I may know Him and the power of His resurrection, and the fellowship of His sufferings, being conformed to His death, if, by any means, I may attain to the resurrection from the dead". He explained his great desire to know the Saviour, who showed him such love, and to live in the power of His resurrection. He knew, too, that this meant having fellowship in His sufferings in a world that rejected Christ, as now. This involved judging the old nature by practically applying Christ's death: being crucified with Christ; also living in the power of new life in Christ. Living so close to his resurrected Saviour and Lord was the reason Paul abounded in the work of the Lord.

After unfolding the power of Christ's resurrection in 1 Corinthians 15, Paul ends the chapter with the marvellous words, "Therefore my beloved brethren. . ." It is wonderful to know we are loved by God and that we are in the family of God. These blessings should provoke in us a desire to serve our Saviour. Interestingly, Paul uses words that convey both stillness and activity to encourage a response in the hearts of his readers. Being "steadfast" is about being fixed and secure in one position. Christ's death and resurrection is the ground on which we spiritually stand, and we are not to be moved from it. The death and resurrection of Christ have been continuously attacked for over 2000 years. In Corinth some denied the resurrection. Today there are those, within the realm of Christendom, who continue to deny it. Paul is absolutely clear that if Christ was not raised then our faith is futile (vv. 16-17), and we are still in our sins because we have no Saviour. But he immediately declares that Christ has been raised from the dead (v. 20). We rest in faith upon the death and resurrection of our Lord Jesus Christ; nothing should move us from this position or from our desire to serve Him.

The Lord Jesus lived here in communion with His Father in heaven, and He abounded in the work the Father gave Him to do. We can have a tendency to emphasise worship, or service, as though they were in competition. But they are a harmonious expression of response to God, and one leads to the other; worshippers are workers. The certainty and security we have in Christ should stimulate us to be always abounding in the work of the Lord. The work includes "whatever you do in word or deed, do all in the name of the Lord Jesus, giving thanks to God the Father through Him" (Colossians 3:17). And we should do such work willingly and joyfully: "Whatever you do, do it heartily, as to the Lord and not to men" (Colossians 3:23). Paul assures his readers that our work is not fruitless, and the Lord values and will use what we do for Him. We should never forget that the God who numbers the hairs on our heads and keeps our tears in a bottle measures perfectly, not only what we do for Him, but the devotion with which we do it. He values our response to our risen Saviour; abounding grace produces abounding worshippers and workers.

Day 59

The still small voice

Do not fret—it only causes harm. (Psalm 37:8)

When I was a child, my mum and grandmother would often say "Don't fret." I grew up instinctively knowing what it meant: "Don't worry; it will be alright." This word 'fret' has two meanings: to be always anxious, and to gradually wear away something. It is a powerful word. Worry can eat away at our lives and drain us of peace and energy. We encourage each other in trying circumstances, but the reality is that we are often overcome by situations, and some of these do not change. So, how do we manage when we are faced with debilitating worry and anxiety? Is it too simple to say, "Don't fret; it will be alright"? Well, it depends on who is saying it.

When we are children, and we have an accident or things go wrong, we go to those who love us to put it right. But sometimes we hide the problem, out of feelings of failure, guilt or independence. As Christians, we can follow the same patterns of behaviour. We go in faith to the Lord; or, we carry our burdens. A dear friend of mine went with his uncle, a man who taught me much about the Christian life, to visit relatives in Norway. On the flight, he told his uncle he had not been able to sleep the night before and had tried counting sheep. His uncle replied, "Next time you can't sleep, don't count sheep talk to the shepherd." He didn't say this just because it was a catchy way to remember our need to turn to the Lord in prayer. He said it because he believed it. He was a man who had learned, not merely to ask God for things, but to walk contentedly in communion with the Lord.

Burdens come to two forms: those the Lord asks us to carry, and those we choose to carry. We learn to distinguish between the two, and how to deal with care, in the presence of God. The Lord has told us in unmistakable terms not to fret, but to cast all our care upon Him (1 Peter 5:7). It takes real faith to do this. We often come to God, without realising it, on our own terms and with our own expectations of what we want Him to do. We focus on the problem that hurts us, when God wants us to focus on Him – the God who heals us (Exodus 15:26). In doing so, everything else falls into place.

Elijah helps us to understand how we learn not to fret. The prophet had witnessed so powerfully to the power of God. But, in 1 Kings 19:11-13, he stood before God, full of despair and loneliness. God sent a great and strong wind, an earthquake and then a fire. It was in such displays of power that Elijah expected to find God. But the Lord was not in the wind, the earthquake or the fire. And in the quietness which followed, he heard a still small voice (a low whisper).

I never cease to be amazed by how the Lord reveals His all-mighty power in stillness and smallness. He holds this tiny world in the vastness of the universe. The Lord Jesus entered this world He made and displayed His supernatural power to demonstrate who He was. This led to the full revelation of the love, mercy and grace of God in His death at Calvary and His glorious resurrection. It was through suffering and sacrifice that the Lord Jesus manifests the heart of God. He did this to bring us to Himself and for us to find in Him every resource. We look at problems, and want to experience God's powerful intervention at our time of need. The response we are looking for is found in the closeness, peace and power of His presence and in hearing His transforming voice say, "Do not fret."

Day 60

Wednesday

Help my unbelief

Immediately the father of the child cried out and said with tears,
"Lord, I believe; help my unbelief!"   (Mark 9:24)

Repetition is vital to learning. Some of you may remember at school reciting aloud our "times tables" or writing out the word "necessary" fifty times (I hope I have spelt it correctly!). God never ceases to remind us to trust Him. In the 21st century He still expects us to live by faith. This trust in Him is not only for times of crisis but for every day of our lives. Trust is something which grows. As we learn to trust the Lord in ordinary circumstances, so we learn to trust Him in extraordinary circumstances. Trust is about a relationship. There is a joy in trusting God because it demonstrates our relationship with Him. It is the experience of throwing ourselves into the arms of God and discovering that

> "The eternal God is your refuge,
> And underneath are the everlasting arms"
> (Deuteronomy 33:27).

When we first came in all our need and in simple faith to the Saviour, we experienced the wonder of God's love and peace and the joy it brought to our hearts. It is strange, then, that after such an experience, we would hesitate to trust the One who so transformed our lives. Yet this does happen. Often the Lord Jesus had to rebuke His disciples' lack of faith. Their unbelief was irrational because they witnessed the power of the Saviour in every circumstance, yet when the storm came, or they faced a crowd of hungry people, their faith retreated. I have to confess to experiencing my faith fleeing in the same way.

In Mark 9 a father comes to the Lord to ask Him to heal his mute son: "But if You can do anything, have compassion on us and help us" (Mark 9:22). He just wanted help. I have noticed that in public prayer we often use the expression, "Lord, we just want…" We set our sights low; we only want some help. It seems we are uncertain about asking for more, probably because we don't feel worthy or deserving. The Lord addresses this problem. Even though the father was distressed, Jesus presses him: "If you can believe, all things are possible to him who believes." Why does the Lord sometimes add pressure when we are already under pressure? Because He wants to take us to the place of utter trust. This pressure produced the father's powerful and honest response: "Lord, I believe; help my unbelief!" (v. 24).

The father expresses what it means to trust God. Twice he uses the word "help". In Hebrews 4:16 we read, "Let us therefore come boldly to the throne of grace, that we may obtain mercy and find grace to help in time of need." The father had travelled in a short time from a place where he asked the Lord Jesus, "If you can help?" to throwing himself into the arms of God.

Tears can express sorrow or joy. They also express great need; we break down when we have a deep sense of our complete weakness. Trust is about sensing our weakness but, at the same time, appealing to the One who can answer all our need. The father recognised the Lord's person and power, and believed, "Lord, I believe." He also understood how fragile his faith was and appealed to the Lord for help to trust Him. We don't think enough about this. Even when we are trusting, we worry that our faith will fail, thinking everything depends on us. The power of the father's faith was not only that he believed the Lord could heal his son, but that he called on the Lord to remove the unbelief his circumstances generated. It was a prayer that moved the heart of Christ; it still does.

Day 61

Thursday

The Son of God who loved me

I have been crucified with Christ; it is no longer I who live, but Christ lives in me; and the life which I now live in the flesh I live by faith in the Son of God, who loved me and gave Himself for me.   (Galatians 2:20)

By the time Paul wrote his letter to the Galatians he had been a Christian for around twenty years. During that time he had preached the Gospel continuously and ministered to the church of Christ. In his letter he reaffirms this Gospel and repels those who attempted to undermine it through a return to the Mosaic law and withering legalism. Such beliefs were self-centred and self-righteous. Over the centuries, the law powerfully demonstrated our inability to meet its demands and proved our need for salvation through the grace of God. He writes in ch. 2:16: "that we might be justified by faith in Christ and not by the works of the law; for by the works of the law no flesh shall be justified".

Through the Holy Spirit, Paul dismantled the teaching, which opposed the grace and love of God. Such thinking is still present with us today and enslaves people in fruitless efforts to reach up to God. But in ch. 2:20, Paul does not present detailed and complicated explanations. He speaks from his heart as he focuses on what had changed and overwhelmed his life: the love of Christ. Paul preached about this love ceaselessly and led so many to salvation. But in this verse he pauses to wonder afresh at the astonishing fact that the Son of God loved *him*. He had once believed, in all the pride and self-will that then filled his life, that God could not fail to accept him. This all changed on the road to Damascus. The Lord stooped from the glory of heaven to say those simple words: "I am Jesus." He emptied Saul's heart of all its darkness, delusion, and violent sinfulness, and He filled it with the love that is stronger than death.

Years later, after witnessing in others the unbelief that once engulfed him, Paul writes: "The Son of God ... loved me and gave Himself for me." This love was the driving force of Paul's life, and he could not keep it to himself. His words capture the majesty of Christ's love. It is one thing to know Jesus is the Saviour of the world, but another to know that He loved and died for me. Paul expressed this love in his preaching of the Gospel, ministry of the whole counsel of God, and in making tents. Paul lived in the present reality and wonder of the Saviour's sacrifice for him, and it stimulated and directed his witness and worship. On the cross, as Jesus was dying for the whole world, He brought a dying thief to Himself. In doing so, He was teaching us what Paul writes, "the Son of God who loved me and gave Himself for me". There will be a countless host of the redeemed in heaven, and every single person will be there because Jesus loved and gave Himself for every one of us. We are never a crowd of faces to God. He sees the one flock and knows every single one of us by name. The love of the Father and the Son and the power of the Spirit of God ensure our eternal security.

> "My sheep hear My voice, and I know them, and they follow Me. And I give them eternal life, and they shall never perish; neither shall anyone snatch them out of My hand. My Father, who has given them to Me, is greater than all; and no one is able to snatch them out of My Father's hand. I and My Father are one" (John 10:27-30).

Whatever circumstances we pass through, however deeply our faith is challenged, and our weakness felt, one thing remains constant, unchanging and victorious: "The Son of God loved me and gave Himself for me."

Day 62

The supply of all our needs

And my God shall supply all your need according to His riches in glory by Christ Jesus. Now to our God and Father be glory forever and ever. Amen. (Philippians 4:19-20)

Early in the 20th century, two brothers decided to emigrate to America. It took them a long time to save the money for the tickets, but the day came when they embarked on the journey across the Atlantic Ocean with great excitement. They took provisions with them and made them last for the whole of the crossing. The night before they landed in New York, they decided to go to the restaurant and buy a meal. At the entrance they asked the man at the door how much a meal would cost. The man asked for their tickets. They produced them. He inspected the tickets and, returning them, said, "All your meals are included on your ticket!" They had travelled the whole of the journey and not realised everything they needed was provided. The brother who recounted this story was making the point that we often go through our lives not taking full advantage of what Paul writes in Philippians 4:19: "And my God shall supply all your need according to His riches in glory by Christ Jesus."

If we were not told, we would never guess as we read Ephesians, Philippians, Colossians and Philemon that Paul was imprisoned. There was no sense of confinement as he wrote of Christ's love in Ephesians; Christ's joy in Philippians; Christ's glory in Colossians and Christ's forgiveness in Philemon. His ministry is so full of the Person of Christ and His riches in glory. He did not say *God* would supply all the needs of the saints in Philippi but, "*My* God shall supply..." He wrote about something he was in the enjoyment of, and that he wanted all the people of God to enjoy. David wrote at the beginning of Psalm 23:

> The LORD is My shepherd;
> I shall not want.

He added in v. 5:

> My cup runs over.

God's grace and mercy abounds towards us in Christ. I think, if we could have visited Paul in prison, we would have come away with our hearts lifted up to Christ in glory and our faith energised to serve Him on earth.

In the Old Testament, Joseph endured enormous suffering. During his time in prison he served Pharaoh's cupbearer and butler. The morning after their strange dreams, Joseph says to them, "Why do you look so sad today?" (Genesis 40:7). Incredibly Joseph, despite his suffering, lived so cheerfully through his imprisonment and also recognised and ministered to the distress of others. Why? Because God was with him. God was with Paul in prison. This transformed his circumstances. Paul did not look inward. Twenty years earlier, God had used Paul's imprisonment in Philippi to form the assembly there. He never ceased wanting them to know the wonder of their every need being supplied by God in Christ. And as he encouraged them in this, his imprisonment could not prevent his heart soaring in worship.

Our two friends never read their tickets! Let us not arrive in heaven the same way. Let us not miss the joyful experience of walking with the Lord, knowing day by day the wonder of the riches of His grace, the supply of every need and the joy of worship.

"Now to our God and Father be glory forever and ever. Amen."

Day 63

Saturday

A brick wall

---

*Remember Jesus Christ, risen from the dead, the offspring of
David, as preached in my gospel, for which I am suffering, bound
with chains as a criminal. But the word of God is not bound!*

(2 Timothy 2:8-9, ESV)

A young bricklayer in Italy was desperate to leave the Christian
home he had grown up in. When the opportunity to work in
another town presented itself, he could not wait to get away.
As he was about to leave, his mother tried to give him a Bible,
but her son told her in no uncertain terms that he did believe
the Bible and didn't want her gift. Although his mother was
heartbroken, she took the opportunity to slip the Bible into her
son's work bag. A few days later, he found the Bible amongst his
tools. His first job was to build an internal wall in a house. As
he was about to finish the task, he turned to his workmates and,
showing them the Bible, said, "My mother believes this book is
the living word of God, but I am going to ensure it is of no use
to anyone." Then, taking the Bible, he hid it behind the bricks
of the wall and sealed it up.

A few years later, after a drinking session, the young man and
his friends were walking home through the local market. He
stopped at a stall selling Bibles and Christian books. He asked
the stallholder if he believed the Bible was the living word of
God. The Christian stallholder assured him he did. The young
man laughed and told the story of how he had hidden the Bible
given to him in the wall of a house. "What good," he asked the
Christian, "would that Bible do?" The man could not believe
his ears and asked him which house it was. The young man

described the house in the area he had worked in. The Christian said it was his house. He explained that, when he demolished a wall to extend his home, he discovered a Bible. He began reading it, and it led him to Jesus Christ. He explained he was trying to share his faith with other people through his bookstall. The young bricklayer became furious and attacked the man with his friends and ran off. The following day as the stallholder lay recovering in hospital, his attacker walked into the ward and to his bedside. He was broken-hearted and full of regret, and sought the forgiveness of the Christian. In the conversation which followed, he opened his heart to the Lord Jesus.

There are many, many Christian parents whose hearts have been broken by their children's rejection of the Saviour. Many Christians feel deep distress over loved ones, friends and neighbours they have sought to lead to Christ. This is compounded when it involves those who, in the words of the Apostle, "were running so well" yet now appear to have no interest in the Saviour they once followed. We feel our weakness, and we regret mistakes we made in the bringing up of our children or in the communicating of our faith.

But never let our broken hearts cause despair. The love we feel comes from the heart of Christ. Reproach and rejection broke His heart. But He never ceases to break down the walls people erect in resistance to the love of God. Sometimes He breaks down such barriers suddenly, as He did with Saul of Tarsus and the Philippian jailor, and at other times it takes a lifetime, and we may never see it. His love does not fail, and we should take refuge in it. But that love should also instil in us holy confidence in what the Lord can do. He can act in power and grace to save, recover and restore those who mean so much to us, and even more to Him. We can appeal in faith to Him to do what seems impossible. And we can take every opportunity to act as He would act in continuing to reach out to those we love, in expectation of their blessing.

Day 64

Sunday

Overflowing hearts

Then she (the queen of Sheba) gave the king one hundred and twenty talents of gold, spices in great quantity, and precious stones. There never again came such abundance of spices as the queen of Sheba gave to King Solomon. (1 Kings 10:10)

When the wise men came to Jesus and presented gifts of gold, frankincense, and myrrh, their hearts were overflowing with joy. When Mary anointed Jesus with a pound of very costly oil of spikenard, her heart overflowed in worship. When Nicodemus came with myrrh and aloes, and Mary Magdalene and Mary the mother of James, and Salome came with spices, their hearts overflowed with sorrow. When the Lord appeared in resurrection, their sorrows were removed, and their hearts overflowed with joy and worship. The disciples of the Lord were moved to respond to the Saviour's suffering death upon the cross and then entered into the joy of knowing that the Saviour had conquered death to enter into His glory.

None of the disciples came empty-handed. What they brought was an expression of how much the Lord meant to them. Their gifts were precious, costly, carefully chosen and freely given from worshipping hearts. They were also given with reverence and humility. The wise men fell down to worship the Lord when He was born. Mary worshipped at the feet of Jesus as His death approached. It is only in the hearts of the Lord's people that the Lord receives gratitude and praise and His love is recognised.

The worship came silently from hearts overwhelmed by grace. And the Lord filled their hearts with His love, peace, joy and hope. The Lord never ceases to value the worship that comes from those for whom He gave Himself. We learn much from the simple response of those who witnessed and responded to the death of Christ. It was an experience that broke their hearts. John later wrote of the apostles: "That which was from the beginning, which we have heard, which we have seen with our eyes, which we have looked upon, and our hands have handled, concerning the Word of life." But it was not the apostles who handled the Lord in death; it was two secret disciples, Joseph and Nicodemus. And it was not the apostles who were there at the tomb of the Lord very early in the morning while it was still dark; it was Mary Magdalene, Mary the mother of James, and Salome. Those who are forgiven much love much.

It is the memory of the depth of Christ's love for us and the power and majesty of His glorious life which bows our hearts in profound worship and stimulates our devotion to Him and service for Him. When we come to remember Him, we bring of our personal experience and appreciation of His Person and His grace, mercy and love. These experiences distil worship in our hearts. Sometimes we are overcome, as the Queen of Sheba was when she saw the glory of Solomon and "there was no more spirit in her" (1 Kings 10:5). But the Queen of Sheba also responded from an overflowing heart: "There never again came such abundance of spices as the queen of Sheba gave to King Solomon." In eternity we shall fully express the worthiness of our Lord and Saviour Jesus Christ. That song begins in our hearts now.

Day 65

Trust, do good, dwell, feed and delight

Do not fret because of evildoers,
Nor be envious of the workers of iniquity.
For they shall soon be cut down like the grass,
And wither as the green herb.
Trust in the LORD, and do good;
Dwell in the land, and feed on His faithfulness.
Delight yourself also in the LORD,
And He shall give you the desires of your heart.   *(Psalm 37:1-4)*

I have always appreciated Psalm 37. The opening verses are a helpful way to approach each day. The Psalm begins by telling us not to be anxious about the evil we see in the world. It doesn't say we shouldn't care or be concerned about its effects, but that we should not worry. It reminds us that this world and its judgment are in the hands of God. There is a peace in knowing that ultimately God will address all this world's ills in perfect righteousness. But the Psalmist is concerned about how we should live in such circumstances, and he encourages us to "trust in the Lord, and do good". There is a great simplicity in this Psalm that provides us with a clear spiritual pathway. The Psalm focuses our faith on the Lord and, in doing so, equips us to do good. The Lord will guide us each day in "paths of righteousness" (Psalm 23:3) and enable us to follow the One who "went about doing good" (Acts 10:38).

The Psalm then encourages us to "dwell in the land, and feed on His faithfulness". Of course, the Psalmist was thinking of God's people dwelling in the physical land He had given them and enjoying His great faithfulness, which was new every morning.

For us, it is an illustration of possessing all the spiritual blessings we have in Christ. These include His love, mercy and grace towards us, our salvation, sanctification and the hope we have in Christ. These spiritual blessings are to be known and enjoyed, and should empower us. And God's faithfulness to us in Christ encourages and sustains our daily trust in Him:

> The steadfast love of the LORD never ceases;
> his mercies never come to an end;
> they are new every morning;
> great is your faithfulness. (Lamentations 3:22-23, ESV)

But then he adds,

> Delight yourself also in the LORD,
> And He shall give you the desires of your heart.

The focus here is on the Lord Himself. The essence of communion is delighting in the Lord. It is what the Saviour meant by "Abide in Me" (John 15:4), and what Paul meant when he said, "that I may know Him" (Philippians 3:10). This experience shapes our desires.

God speaks of giving us the desires of our hearts. But He anticipates those desires being in harmony with His perfect will and purposes. We can act in opposition to the will of God and desire things outside of that will. In such circumstances, God may allow us to have what we want and send leanness to our souls (Psalm 106:15). But God wants the best for us, and we learn this in His presence. It is in His presence we learn to trust Him and are prepared for service. It is where we can reflect on our blessings and are encouraged by His promises and great faithfulness. Most of all, it is where we experience the glory and the grace of the Person who is our Saviour. Knowing and delighting in Christ transforms us into the people God wants us to be. Communion with Christ makes us Christlike.

Day 66

Barnabas, sacrificing and serving

And Joses, who was also named Barnabas by the apostles (which is translated Son of Encouragement), a Levite of the country of Cyprus, having land, sold it, and brought the money and laid it at the apostles' feet. (Acts 4:36-37)

In the last chapter of John's Gospel the Lord speaks to Peter about shepherding His sheep (John 21:15-19). Towards the end of his life Peter writes about the characteristics needed to be a shepherd of the flock of God (1 Peter 5:1-4). And I think, to help us further in understanding this vital ministry, the Spirit of God gave us the example of a man who had the heart of a true shepherd; his name was Barnabas.

We are introduced to him at a critical moment in the history of the early Church – just before the sin of covetousness marred the remarkable testimony of the people of God in Acts 5. We can look further back and see the damage this sin did in the days of Joshua (Joshua 7), and Paul writes in Colossians 3:5, "covetousness, which is idolatry". In contrast, Barnabas sold his land and brought the money to the apostles for use in the service of God. It wasn't merely a gift; it was an expression of his desire to give his life entirely to the service of God. God loves a cheerful giver, and the apostles gave him the name "Son of Encouragement".

When Saul of Tarsus, following his conversion, attempted to join the disciples at Jerusalem, he was still seen as an enemy (Acts 9:26-27). It was Barnabas who befriended him, brought him to the apostles and spoke on his behalf. This gives us an insight into the shepherd-heart of Barnabas. He cared for God's people, he saw value in them when others did not, and he defended and encouraged them in their faith and service.

A great persecution of the Christians at Jerusalem followed the death of Stephen. It led, by God's grace, to the Gospel spreading to Samaria in Acts 8 and to Antioch in Acts 11. Astonishingly, the Lord used the death of Stephen to spread the Gospel through the lives both of ordinary disciples and of gifted servants of God. God lit a fire in their hearts, and despite their suffering, they communicated the love of God everywhere they went. When the apostles heard of the blessing at Antioch, they sent Barnabas to encourage them. The apostles held Barnabas in high regard and knew he would benefit those he was sent to serve.

I think Barnabas' arrival in Antioch gives us an excellent lesson in shepherding the people of God. Barnabas didn't rush to organise or direct or even teach. As a true shepherd, he looked over the flock of God, he saw the grace of God, and he was glad. In serving God's people, we should never be superficial or hasty. We should time take to see the ways God's grace has moved in the hearts of His people, and we should rejoice in it. Whatever the problems Paul had to deal with amongst the churches he sought to serve, he always began with what the grace of God had done in their lives. I wonder if he learned that from Barnabas, who built on what God had already done. In the King James Version, we read that he "exhorted them all, that with purpose of heart they would cleave unto the Lord" (Acts 11:23). I love the word "cleave"; here it means "to adhere firmly and closely or loyally and unwaveringly to something". Barnabas crystallises the blessing and power of the Christian life with these simple words: stay close to the Lord.

Day 67

Wednesday

Barnabas, a good man, full of the Holy Spirit and of faith

For he was a good man, full of the Holy Spirit and of faith. And a great many people were added to the Lord. Then Barnabas departed for Tarsus to seek Saul. And when he had found him, he brought him to Antioch. So it was that for a whole year they assembled with the church and taught a great many people. And the disciples were first called Christians in Antioch.

(Acts 11:24-26)

In a few words, the Holy Spirit tells us so much about Barnabas:

He was a good man. Barnabas did not have mixed motives or self-interest; he genuinely sought the blessing of others. His goodness was a result of the work of God in his life. The early church prospered because those within it were transformed by the love of Christ into His likeness. Christ transformed Zaccheus, the tax collector, into the most generous of men. Paul said to the Philippian jailor, "Believe on the Lord Jesus Christ and you will be saved" (Acts 16:31), and the heartless jailer was transformed into the gentlest of men. Barnabas was who he was because of Christ's work in him.

He was full of the Holy Spirit. Paul writes in Ephesians 5:18: "And do not be drunk with wine, in which is dissipation; but be filled with the Spirit." He compares the loss of control and damage caused by drunkenness with the fruitfulness and blessing of a life filled with the Holy Spirit of God. Being filled with the Holy Spirit is being like Jesus. Through the Holy Spirit, we are characterised by love, joy, peace, longsuffering, kindness, goodness and the other features of the fruit of the Spirit. The Holy Spirit's ministry is to glorify Christ in and through us. Barnabas was filled with and empowered by the Spirit of God to minister Christ and to care for His people.

He was also full of faith. He had faith to sell his land; he had faith to befriend and encourage Saul, and he had faith to share the Gospel and nurture the people of God in Jerusalem and Antioch. His faith in God was expressed in the reality of daily life. He walked with God and had complete confidence in what God could do. He encouraged the Lord's people to "cleave to the Lord with purpose of heart", because that's how he lived. Like Peter, he became a shepherd of the flock of God because he knew the Good Shepherd and understood how important it was to be an example to the flock of God (1 Peter 5:3). And his ministry was also evangelistic. A large number of people were led to the Lord. A true shepherd always seeks to lead people to Christ for their salvation and their sanctification.

Barnabas also had a rare quality. He saw so clearly the grace of God in the lives of his fellow believers. Barnabas was a guileless man who discerned, encouraged and valued gift and ability in others. He left Antioch to seek, find and bring Saul to help in the work of God in the city. This is a description of a shepherd, not finding a lost sheep, but finding a valuable servant of God and bringing him to a place where he was needed. A faithful pastor not only ministers to the needs of God's people but values and stimulates them to use their spiritual gift. Barnabas brought Saul into a place where his gift would be a blessing to others, and he rejoiced in working with him. Their harmonious Christ-centred ministry led to the disciples being called Christians for the first time. Barnabas' simple appeal to his fellow believers to "stay close to the Lord" had a transforming influence. It still should.

Day 68

Barnabas, a fellow servant and a friend

---

*Now in the church that was at Antioch there were certain
prophets and teachers: Barnabas, Simeon who was called Niger,
Lucius of Cyrene, Manaen who had been brought up with Herod
the tetrarch, and Saul. As they ministered to the Lord and fasted,
the Holy Spirit said, "Now separate to Me Barnabas and Saul for
the work to which I have called them."*   *(Acts 13:1-2)*

Barnabas had a prominent role faithfully serving the Lord in
Jerusalem, Antioch and in the first missionary journeys. The
spiritual partnership he formed with Paul was of enormous
blessing to the Church of Christ. At the end of Acts 11 they were
trusted to take relief for the brethren in Judea (Acts 11:27-30),
and, after fulfilling this ministry, they returned with John Mark
to Antioch. Interestingly, Scripture records their faithfulness
in the spiritual and also the practical care of the people of
God before their call by the Holy Spirit: "Now separate to Me
Barnabas and Saul for the work to which I have called them."

Acts 13 and 14 are a testimony to harmony in the service of
God. Barnabas and Saul, two spiritual and gifted men, blended
together so effectively in fulfilling a shared ministry. It can
be challenging to share a ministry, and I think it helped that
they were friends. We should never underestimate the value
of true Christian friendship, and choose our friends wisely. As
the unique ministry of Paul as a "chosen vessel" (Acts 9:15)
begins to emerge in these chapters, there is no evidence that
Barnabas became jealous of his friend Saul, who is later called
Paul. The theme of their ministry in Antioch continued into
their missionary work, as they encouraged disciples to continue

in the grace of God (Acts 13:43). Together they were led of the Spirit to reach out to the Gentiles with the Gospel (Acts 13:46) and together they suffered persecution (Acts 13:50). In Acts 14, after Paul healed a man crippled from birth at Lystra, Barnabas and Paul were regarded as gods and, horrified by this reaction, they appealed to the people to turn to the living God. But, interestingly, Barnabas was called Zeus and Paul Hermes, because he was the chief speaker (Acts 14:12). Barnabas did not heal, nor was he the principal speaker, but his spiritual bearing had an impact on the people. Barnabas' calm and caring character endeared him to the apostles, the people of God in Jerusalem and Antioch, to his friend Paul and to the people of Lystra. Barnabas and Paul present the harmony of the character and message of the Christian faith.

Jews from Antioch and Iconium arrived and stirred up persecution, which resulted in the stoning of Paul. But the two friends continued in their ministry of preaching, strengthening, encouraging, fasting and praying, and establishing elders on the return journey to Antioch where they had begun.

This first missionary journey was a witness to the leading, power and presence of the Holy Spirit in the work of God. It teaches us about the different gifts and abilities of God's servants. We learn to serve God, not in competition with one another, but by valuing and encouraging each other. We are given examples of how to work in harmony, and being enabled to reach out with the Gospel in difficult places, and to strengthen and build up the Lord's people. How did Barnabas and Paul do all of this? By "staying close to the Lord". When we are close to the Lord, then we are closest to each other, and everything comes into focus.

Day 69

Barnabas, a pastor

---

*Now Barnabas was determined to take with them John called
Mark. But Paul insisted that they should not take with them the
one who had departed from them in Pamphylia, and had not
gone with them to the work. Then the contention became so sharp
that they parted from one another.* (*Acts 15:37-39*)

After all the blessing of Acts 13 and 14, chapter 15 does not
start well. Men arrived in Antioch from Jerusalem determined
to undermine the grace of God by insisting on circumcision
being necessary for salvation. Paul and Barnabas forcefully
resisted this false teaching. This led them with other brethren to
Jerusalem. At the Jerusalem Council the matter was settled by
the witness of Peter, Barnabas, Paul and the judgement of James
(Acts 15:6-21). This was communicated to the churches in a
letter which referred to "beloved Barnabas and Paul, men who
have risked their lives for the name of our Lord Jesus Christ"
(vv. 25-26).

After returning to Antioch, Paul is exercised to revisit the
brethren he and Barnabas had ministered amongst, to see how
they were progressing (v. 36). It is important to distinguish
between the direct calling of the Holy Spirit in Acts 13:2, and
Paul's personal exercise. (This personal exercise led to another
direct calling from the Holy Spirit in chapter 16:6-10.) Barnabas
was willing to go with Paul, but wanted to take John Mark, who
had gone on their first missionary journey (Acts 13:5) but left
to return to Jerusalem (Acts 13:13). Paul doubted his suitability
for similar service.

So these two great men of God and close friends disagreed about John Mark and went their separate ways. Paul's remarkable service is outlined by Luke in the rest of the Book of Acts, and Barnabas goes with John Mark to Cyprus. Barnabas understood that, when we serve God, He is not only working through us, He is working in us. Paul would later write about what he had learned whilst serving God (Philippians 4:10-13). Barnabas had taken Paul and introduced him to the apostles, and he had left Antioch to find Paul and include him in the valuable ministry in that city. He cared about individuals and their spiritual progress. So he personally took responsibility for John Mark. Paul viewed the work of God in its extensiveness: Barnabas was seeking the restoration of a failed servant. Some think that Barnabas was influenced by his family relationship (see Colossians 4:10). This thinking belittles his character, but would to God that we all had such a deep interest in the spiritual welfare of our relatives. The children of the saints can suffer from spiritual neglect.

But Barnabas was following the Lord's example. Thomas wilfully rejected the news of the resurrection of Christ, and the Lord restored him. Peter denied the Lord Jesus three times, yet the Lord did not stop him serving, but restored and called him to be a shepherd. John Mark failed the Lord in service, but ultimately the Lord called him to write the Gospel of Mark, the Gospel that speaks of Jesus as the Servant of God. Paul did not need Barnabas, but John Mark did. And the young man who went with Barnabas to Cyprus became the servant of God Paul refers to in some of the last words he wrote: "Get Mark and bring him with you, for he is useful to me for ministry" (2 Timothy 4:11). I wonder if Paul saw at the end of his life the devotion to service and the friendship he shared with Barnabas in his younger fellow-servants, Timothy and John Mark respectively. We need the vision and purpose of servants like Paul, and we need the hearts of pastors like Barnabas, who would always keep us close to the Lord.

Day 70

The Book of Life, the heart of joy, the peace of God

Whose names are in the Book of Life.   (Philippians 4:3)

Rejoice in the Lord always. Again I will say, rejoice!   (4:4)

The peace of God, which surpasses all understanding.   (4:7)

The final chapter of Philippians is so uplifting. Paul demonstrates the reality of his ministry in his own life and at the same time desires so much that his fellow Christians might share in his experience. This desire came out of the genuine love he had for the church at Philippi. In the first chapter of the letter, Paul writes "I have you in my heart." All service is the overflow of the love Christ has for us.

Today we hear a lot about the can-do attitude demonstrated in a determination to accept and overcome life's challenges. Paul had a can-do approach 2000 years ago: it did not have its source in himself, but in Christ. He saw his weakness, and the means through which Christ could demonstrate His power. This is why he starts the chapter, "stand fast in the Lord". This extraordinary powerful and joyous letter was written from prison by an Apostle who, after years of service and suffering, stood firm in His faith in the Lord Jesus Christ and appealed to the Philippians to do the same. What follows is very practical. He first deals with a problem between two sisters and entreats them to agree in the Lord, reminding them of the way they had served the Lord together. He asks the saints to help them resolve their problem. He reminds them of the love of Christ, which had placed their names side by side in the Book of Life.

Such love dissolves disagreement and restores the joy of our fellowship of love in Christ.

Then Paul returns to one of the consistent themes of his letter: joy. I remember being told of a brother who stood outside his church every Sunday evening and faithfully distributed tracts to passers-by. He always dressed in a dark suit and had a solemn face. One evening, he offered a tract to a man, who refused it with the words, "No thank you, I have enough problems!" Joy is placed after love in the features of the fruit of the Spirit. Christ's love puts our names in the Book of Life. The same love fills our hearts with joy: "Rejoice in the Lord always. Again I will say, rejoice!" (v. 4). Joy is not merely a feeling. There is energy in joy. Sadness weakens us, but joy strengthens us. The joy of the Lord is our strength. It was joy in the burning hearts of the two disciples who had walked all the way to Emmaus that gave them the power to get up and walk all the way back to Jerusalem. Paul associates joy with the gentleness of Christ, and with the nearness of the Lord both now and in the assurance of His return (v. 5).

Paul goes on to encourage his readers to bring everything to the Lord in prayer with thanksgiving. It is through the practice of prayer we know the peace of God, "which passes all understanding". The peace of God guards and protects our hearts and minds in Christ. It removes anxiety, focuses our minds on what is positive and brings us close to the God of peace. In these brief opening verses of the final chapter of Philippians, Paul conveys his enjoyment of the light of love, joy and peace, which streamed into his prison cell. It was an experience he could not keep to himself; it had to be shared. And we are so thankful to the Lord that it is shared with us.

Day 71

The prayer of Jesus

Father, I desire that they also whom You gave Me may be with Me where I am, that they may behold My glory which You have given Me; for You loved Me before the foundation of the world.

(John 17:24)

In John 17:1, as the cross loomed before Him, the Son of God prayed to God the Father: "Glorify Your Son, that Your Son also may glorify You." The first mention of love in the Bible is not a man's love for a woman; it is a father's love for his son. We discover this in the opening verses of Genesis 22. We are told of the journey Abraham and Isaac took to the land of Moriah. And we learn of a father's sacrifice and the love and devotion of Isaac as he submitted himself to the will of his father. Although Isaac was never sacrificed, he remains a remarkable illustration of Christ, in love, undertaking the Father's will in the work of salvation. Christ's love for the Father is seen in His life of service and in His sacrificial death. The Father's love for the Son is seen in Christ's resurrection and glorification.

It is in all the wonder this love that we see the Lord Jesus has His Church upon His heart. Jesus had kept His disciples during His earthly ministry, and He prayed for them to continue to be held in the love of God as He returned to heaven: "I come to You Holy Father, keep through Your name those whom You have given Me, that they may be one as We are" (vv. 11-12). He did not pray for them to be taken out of the world. Instead, He asked the Father to keep and sanctify them by the word of God to be His witnesses in the world (vv. 15-18). The Lord Jesus also prayed for future generations of Christians: "I do not pray for these alone, but also for those who will believe in Me through their word; that they all may be one, as You, Father, are in Me, and I in You; that they also may be one in Us, that the world may believe that You sent Me" (vv. 20-23). He prayed for you and me.

The culmination of the love of Christ is described in verse 24: "Father, I desire that they also whom You gave Me may be with Me where I am, that they may behold My glory which You have given Me; for You loved Me before the foundation of the world." The incredible journey of divine love which began in eternity, and was fully expressed in this world, led back to glory. And it is the same love of Christ that will ensure one day "we shall always be with the Lord" (1 Thessalonians 4:17).

In Hebrews 12:2-3 we read, "Looking unto Jesus, the author and finisher of our faith, who for the joy that was set before Him endured the cross, despising the shame, and has sat down at the right hand of the throne of God." In John 17, Christ looked beyond the cross to the joy of having His Church in His presence forever. We were in His heart. Today, from heaven, as He looks into this world where he expressed the love of God in His life and in His death, the Lord still embraces the one flock of God within His heart. And He rejoices that we, His people, respond to His love by recalling the pathway that led from glory to the cross. We remember the travail of His soul, and we rejoice in the glory of His resurrection and ascension. By faith, as we look up into heaven to see our risen glorious Lord, He is in our hearts. As we bow in worship to remember Christ's love, we hasten in our hearts the day when we shall be brought by Him into the Father's house (John 14:1-3).

Day 72

The Armour of God: The strength of the Lord and the armour of God

Finally, my brethren, be strong in the Lord and in the power of His might. *(Ephesians 6:10)*

Before Paul describes the armour of God, he focuses our eyes on the Lord. He does this in two ways: first, the Person, then His power. The Person of the Lord is always placed first. So how do we become strong in the Lord? I think Paul helps us to understand this in his letter to the Philippians. In ch. 3:10-11 we read the well-known words: "that I may know Him and the power of His resurrection, and the fellowship of His sufferings, being conformed to His death, if, by any means, I may attain to the resurrection from the dead". Paul explains that knowing the Saviour in His resurrection glory is the source of our strength to live for Him now. We are linked to him by the Holy Spirit. The Spirit's work is to glorify Christ in our hearts and to reproduce the features of Christ in our lives. These features are described in the language of the fruit of the Spirit. We also have the word of God, which sanctifies us, keeping us separate from the world but equipping us to witness in the world (John 17:15-19). But this demands our obedience to the word of God.

Being strong in the Lord enables us draw upon the power of His might. Paul describes this in Philippians 4: 11-13: "I have learned in whatever state I am, to be content: I know how to be abased, and I know how to abound. Everywhere and in all things I have learned both to be full and to be hungry, both to abound and to suffer need. I can do all things through Christ who strengthens me." Paul had learned in all his circumstances that Christ provided the strength he needed. It is this experience he wanted the people of God to know. Only after fixing our eyes on the greatness of the Person and power of the Lord Jesus Christ does the Apostle begin to describe the armour of God.

Great armies need great generals to inspire and empower them. It is not only their equipment that is important, but their commitment to and reliance upon their leaders. Paul encourages us first in our devotion to, and our reliance upon the greatest leader, the Lord Jesus. Then he writes, "Put on the whole armour of God." Paul was used to soldiers because, as a prisoner, he spent a lot of time in their company. He was familiar with their dress and equipment. It was the job of these soldiers to ensure Paul did not escape. But escape was never in Paul's mind. He accepted his circumstances from God and used them to continue serving the Church of Christ. He uses the armour of his captors to vividly illustrate the armour of God. In the very act of doing this, he was demonstrating the supremacy of the Lord Jesus in his own life, which gave him the strength to prove a victorious faith in his own suffering. As he wrote about the armour of God, he was wearing the belt of truth, the breastplate of righteousness, the shoes of the Gospel, the shield of faith, the helmet of salvation, and the sword of the Spirit. Like David when he met Goliath, he faced the enemy, not wearing the cumbersome protection of soldiers in a physical battle, but a heart that looked up to the Saviour and dressed in the invisible armour of truth, righteousness, good news, faith, security and the word of God. This is the armour we all need to put on.

Day 73

Tuesday

The Armour of God: The whole armour of God

Put on the whole armour of God, that you may be able to stand against the wiles of the devil. For we do not wrestle against flesh and blood, but against principalities, against powers, against the rulers of the darkness of this age, against spiritual hosts of wickedness in the heavenly places. Therefore take up the whole armour of God, that you may be able to withstand in the evil day, and having done all, to stand. (Ephesians 6:11-13)

Paul begins in verse 11 by exhorting us to put on the whole armour of God. Although he goes on to describe the separate pieces of armour, these pieces complement each other to form one suit of armour. The purpose of the armour is to enable us to stand. The picture Paul paints is of a soldier facing a dangerous enemy with no thought of retreat. It has been pointed out many times that the armour is all front-facing. He doesn't envisage the soldier running away from the enemy.

Paul then reveals the enemy and the tactics he uses – schemes of deceit. In Revelation 12:9 Satan is called "the deceiver of the whole world". Paul had already warned the Ephesian Christians of "deceitful schemes" (Ephesians 4:14, ESV) which took the form of false teaching. This is not limited to spiritual things but also affects human experience in general. There is an order and plan to the work of Satan and his spiritual forces and the influence he exerts. In Ephesians 2:2, Paul reminded his readers they "once walked according to the course of this world, according to the prince of the power of the air, the spirit who now works in the sons of disobedience". So their enemy was known to them. They had been under his control, but now they were equipped to stand against him.

The apostle's expressions "put on" and "take up" mean 'to put on oneself' and 'to take to oneself'. We are personally encouraged to put on the armour of God, to make it our own and to use. By doing this, we shall be able to stand and to withstand in the evil day. "Standing" implies witness. The evil day is a particular period of trial. The armour of God enables us to stand immovable (see 1 Corinthians 15:58). "Withstanding" is positively pushing back against evil when we are attacked by it. An illustration of this is Shammah who, when everyone fled from a troop of Philistines, "stationed himself in the middle of the field, defended it, and killed the Philistines. So the Lord brought about a great victory" (2 Samuel 23:12).

Today is a day when we need to stand. The rich legacies of the Christian faith are attacked continuously, or eroded, and God's patterns for the well-being of human life abandoned. But we should never be discouraged. God has blessed us with every spiritual blessing. Our life is hidden with Christ in God. We possess eternal life, and we are held in the hands of God the Father and God the Son. The Holy Spirit indwells our hearts. Paul, in the first three chapters of Ephesians, outlines to us God's will, God's work and God's wisdom. In the last three chapters, he writes about the Christian's walk, the Christian's witness and the Christian's warfare. God has made us worshippers and workers. And He has also made us warriors to stand and witness to Him in our generation. Next, Paul goes on to teach us about the armour God has provided for us to be victorious in the spiritual battle we face.

Day 74

The Armour of God: The belt of truth, the breastplate of righteousness and the shoes of the Gospel

Stand therefore, having girded your waist with truth, having put on the breastplate of righteousness and having shod your feet with the preparation of the Gospel of peace. (Ephesians 6:14-15)

The first part of the armour of God is a belt fastened around the waist. Our centre of gravity, when standing, is usually located in front of the sacrum bone, just below the waist. We naturally support ourselves just above this area. The idea of girding is to prepare ourselves for service. The Lord Jesus girded Himself with a towel before undertaking the lowly service of washing the disciples' feet (John 13:4). Paul reminds us that the truth of God is at the basis of all we do. We need to take it in and understand it in our hearts and minds; to make it our own and live by it. God's word and your faith in it are vital. Again, it is the Lord Jesus who demonstrates this. At the outset of His ministry, after His baptism, He goes into the wilderness to confront Satan. He defeats his power by the word of God, the belt of truth. His example is our pattern.

The next piece of armour is the breastplate of righteousness. The breastplate a soldier wore was like a leather waistcoat from the neck to the waist. It was worn primarily to protect his heart and other vital organs, as he stood in battle, but it also covered his back. In the Old Testament, the High Priest wore a breastplate of judgement over his heart. Upon it were twelve stones representing the twelve tribes. It is a beautiful picture of our position before God in Christ, upheld by the power of His love and righteousness. The first thing the father put on the prodigal son when he returned home (Luke 15) was "the best robe", an illustration of the righteousness of Christ placed on us. This is a protection Satan cannot overcome. However, if we live unholy and disobedient lives, we open ourselves up to the attacks of Satan. As Christians, our communion with Christ stimulates our obedience to Him, producing a life consistent with the righteousness we have in Him. This practical expression of righteousness forms our breastplate of righteousness. God alone puts Christ's righteousness on us when we trust in Christ. But we have the responsibility of putting on the breastplate of practical righteousness in our everyday living. Paul adds to this in 1 Thessalonians 5:8 when he writes, "putting on the breastplate of faith and love", encouraging us to live by faith and to show love to one another.

Paul then writes, "having shod your feet with the preparation of the gospel of peace" (v. 15). It is also translated "as shoes for your feet, having put on the readiness given by the gospel of peace" in the ESV. The word used for preparation has the meaning of "readiness" and has also been translated "foundation" in Psalm 89:14 (LXX). Given the apostle's theme of standing, the use of "foundation" is appealing; it fits with the sound footing we have in the Gospel of peace. The upright acacia wood boards overlaid with gold, that formed the structure of the tabernacle, stood on two sockets, or bases, of silver (Exodus 26). This is a powerful illustration of our righteousness in Christ (the gold covering) being based on His death and resurrection (two sockets of silver). We stand on this ground, knowing peace with God, the peace of God and the God of peace. In doing so, we give witness to the power of the Gospel of His grace in our lives: "Always be ready to give a defence to everyone who asks you a reason for the hope that is in you, with meekness and fear" (1 Peter 3:15).

Day 75

The Armour of God: The shield of faith

Above all, taking the shield of faith with which you will be able to quench all the fiery darts of the wicked one. (*Ephesians 6:16*)

The Roman army used several shields, but they developed the large shield which protected the whole body. It was used to defend soldiers from attacks as they advanced. This shield was also designed to fit together with the shields of other soldiers. It provided protection for a unit of soldiers from attacks from all sides and the arrows which could rain down on them. Paul uses this shield to illustrate our trust in God. Satan's objective is to destroy our faith. He continually searches for ways to undermine our confidence in God, knowing that once he can remove our trust in God, we are defeated. That's why Paul writes, "above all, taking the shield of faith". Never let go of your trust in the Saviour, knowing He will never let go of you. Our faith is able to make us victorious in all circumstances. It doesn't take away difficulty; it defeats difficulty.

Jairus came to Jesus and said, "My little daughter lies at the point of death. Come and lay Your hands on her, that she may be healed, and she will live" (Mark 5:23). Jairus had faith in the Lord, and the Lord walked with him to his home. On the way, he stopped to heal the woman with an incurable disease. Afterwards, the news came to Jairus, "Your daughter is dead. Why trouble the Teacher any further?" It was a fiery dart. It was the enemy saying death defeats faith. But on hearing these words, Jesus says to Jairus, "Do not be afraid; only believe." The Lord did not need to take the journey with Jairus. He could have healed his daughter with a word and sent him home rejoicing. In the fourth and fifth chapters of Mark's Gospel, the Lord demonstrates extraordinarily His power over disaster, the devil, disease and finally death. And amid this incredible power, he challenged the faith of His disciples, encouraged Legion to share his story in faith, rejoiced in the faith of the woman who touched his clothes and was healed, and finally strengthens Jairus' faith. He was teaching us to take the shield of faith and face every circumstance trusting Him.

As the stones of hateful men rained down on Stephen in his violent death, he demonstrated – to all of us – the invisible shield of faith. Being full of the Holy Spirit, he had seen the glory of God and Jesus standing at the right hand of God (Acts 7:55-56). The Lord stood by Him as he suffered. He did not need to say to Stephen, "Do not be afraid; only believe." Because Stephen was not afraid, he simply believed in His Saviour, and his heart was full of forgiveness and peace. He held to the very end of his life the shield of faith.

Paul was an accomplice in the death of Stephen when he was martyred. But he was also the subject of Stephen's prayer of faith, "Lord, do not charge them with this sin." And when Paul came to the end of his own life, he was holding the same shield of faith when he wrote, with forgiveness and peace in His heart, "At my first defence no one stood with me, but all forsook me. May it not be charged against them. But the Lord stood with me and strengthened me" (2 Timothy 4:16-17).

The shield of faith will protect us and give us victory in the most trying of circumstances. This victory is not lost, even when we appear to lose everything, because we never lose the love and grace of our Saviour and all that it will accomplish.

Day 76

Friday

The Armour of God: The helmet of salvation and the sword of the Spirit

And take the helmet of salvation, and the sword of the Spirit, which is the word of God. (Ephesians 6:17)

Paul would have been familiar with the Roman imperial helmet. It was designed to protect the whole head. God saves us body, soul and spirit. His salvation embraces every aspect of our lives. Paul earlier described the spiritual battle we are in. He wanted his readers to experience, as he did, the Lord's power of deliverance in this battle by taking "the helmet of salvation". He presses upon us the importance of living day by day in the conscious knowledge and application of God's salvation. In 1 Thessalonians 5:8 Paul adds a further dimension to the helmet. He encourages us to live in the light of Christ's return when he writes about putting on "as a helmet the hope of salvation". Just as the helmet surrounded and protected the head of a soldier, so the salvation we have in Christ Jesus surrounds and protects us.

This is true in regard to sin. We often remind ourselves that we are saved from the penalty (the past), the power (the present) and the presence (the future) of sin. It is also true in regard to the circumstances we face. Paul writes in 2 Timothy 4:17-18: "I was delivered out of the mouth of the lion. And the Lord will deliver me from every evil work and preserve me for His heavenly kingdom. To Him be glory forever and ever. Amen!" The Apostle experienced deliverance from immediate danger, and he believed God would deliver him from future dangers. This experience and faith drew worship from his heart: "To Him be glory forever and ever." God delights to save. Just as at the soldier would place his helmet on his head at the start of his service, Paul encourages us to have complete faith in Christ's saving power as we live for Him day by day.

The helmet protects the head, which represents our minds. In Luke 24:27 (ESV) the Lord Jesus "interpreted to them in all the Scriptures the things concerning himself". Then in verse 45 He "opened their minds to understand the Scriptures". Our minds govern our thinking, our attitudes, our words and our actions. Paul illustrates the connection between the armour we wear and the weapon we hold, the sword of the Spirit, which is the word of God. The word of God, first and foremost, reveals Christ to our hearts and then forms Christ's mind in us. This includes the humility of the mind of Christ that Paul speaks of in Philippians 2 and the obedient mind which rejoiced to do God's will: "Behold, I have come to do your will, O God" (Hebrew 10:7, ESV). God has saved us to express Christ-likeness, and we are equipped to apply the word of God in every circumstance. The word of God is living and powerful (Hebrews 4:12) and the Holy Spirit applies it to our hearts and minds to follow Christ in obedient faith, and to witness to him: "Therefore, my beloved, as you have always obeyed, so now, not only as in my presence but much more in my absence, work out your own salvation with fear and trembling, for it is God who works in you, both to will and to work for his good pleasure" (Philippians 2:12-13).

Day 77

The Armour of God: Prayer

---

*Praying always with all prayer and supplication in the Spirit,
being watchful to this end with all perseverance and supplication
for all the saints— and for me, that utterance may be given to
me, that I may open my mouth boldly to make known the mystery
of the gospel, for which I am an ambassador in chains; that in it I
may speak boldly, as I ought to speak.*   *(Ephesians 6:18-20)*

Paul's teaching on the armour of God begins by looking to
the Lord who is our strength and power. It closes with the
encouragement to look to Him in prayer.

The systematic and spontaneous prayer: "praying always". This
thought embraces the regular times when we pray individually,
in our families and in our prayer meetings, and also includes
being in the spirit of prayer. Nehemiah is an excellent example
of this. When he heard the walls of Jerusalem were destroyed,
he systematically fasted and prayed for many days. Then when
he was sad in the presence of king Artaxerxes, he spontaneously
prayed in his heart to God, and spoke to the king. We are always
close to the throne of God.

The scope of our prayer: "with all prayer". We should be
expansive, simple, focused and straightforward in all our
prayers. But there are also times when we don't know what we
should pray for as we ought. Then the Lord still responds to the
focus and clarity of humble and dependent hearts.

The supplicating character of prayer: "and supplication".
Supplication expresses need in all its forms, recognising that

God supplies all our need according to His riches in glory in Christ, and it leads us to worship (Philippians 4:19-20).

The sanctification of prayer: "in the Spirit". It is the Holy Spirit who guides our prayers and brings them into harmony with the will and purposes of God.

The sightline of prayer: "being watchful to this end". Prayer should be characterised by alertness. We should be watchful and anticipate the spiritual and material needs of ourselves and others (Acts 20:28).

The steadfastness of prayer: "with all perseverance". Prayer is a service. It is thoughtfulness and total commitment.

The saints we pray for: "and supplication for all the saints". No one is excluded. There are those we know and can pray for in detail, but we can also pray for those we know little about who the Lord lays on our hearts.

The servants we pray for: "and for me..." The preaching of the Gospel and those communicating it should always be in our prayers.

Dressed in the armour of God, strong in the Lord and the power of His might, and with hearts lifted in prayer to the throne of God, may we be helped by the Lord to stand together for Him in the times and circumstances He has called us to pass through.

Day 78

Sunday

When stones cry out in worship

Then, as He was now drawing near the descent of the Mount of Olives, the whole multitude of the disciples began to rejoice and praise God with a loud voice for all the mighty works they had seen, saying: "Blessed is the King who comes in the name of the Lord! Peace in heaven and glory in the highest!" And some of the Pharisees called to Him from the crowd, "Teacher, rebuke Your disciples." But He answered and said to them, "I tell you that if these should keep silent, the stones would immediately cry out."
(Luke 19:37-40)

When Jesus was born, not a voice was heard on earth in acknowledgement of the Saviour's birth. But heaven spoke: "And suddenly there was with the angel a multitude of the heavenly host praising God and saying: 'Glory to God in the highest, And on earth peace, goodwill toward men!'" (Luke 2:13-14).

When Jesus entered Jerusalem towards the end of His life on earth, His disciples had His song in their hearts and expressed it loudly and joyfully. The Pharisees did not take part in this joyful praise, and some raised their voices to stop the worship of Christ. The Lord replies with the remarkable words, "I tell you that if these should keep silent, the stones would immediately cry out."

It was on the night of the Lord's betrayal, when the forces of rejection, envy and opposition gathered to plan the destruction of Jesus Christ, that He gave us the simplest expressions of worship: a loaf of bread and cup of wine. He was about to take the final steps to Calvary and, in love, lay down His life for our salvation. Peter was there on that Passover evening, and years later wrote: "Coming to Him as to a living stone, rejected indeed by men, but chosen by God and precious, you also, as living stones, are being built up a spiritual house, a holy priesthood, to offer up spiritual sacrifices acceptable to God through Jesus Christ" (1 Peter 2:4-5).

We hear a lot today about the wonder of the universe as scientists explore its mysteries. As Christians, we see God witnessing to His greatness in the glory of creation. It is not only the heavens which declare the glory of the Lord (Psalm 19:1). His glory is seen in the mountain ranges, oceans, birds, beasts, trees and flowers, rocks and stones, sand on the seashores and in things we need a microscope to see. The whole astonishing complexity of creation witnesses to the glory of God. Yet it is humans, who are so "fearfully and wonderfully" made (Psalm 139:14), who increasingly reject the existence of God and resent and oppose those who do worship Him. The Lord tells us that, failing our praise, the inanimate and simple stone would shame us by crying out in worship.'

It is difficult to think of something so dead as a stone. We once were spiritually dead in trespasses and sins, without hope and without God in the world (Ephesians 2:1,12). But we are now alive in Christ, built upon the Living Stone who suffered rejection and death, but who became the Great Rock of our salvation. Peter explains that, as living stones, we form a spiritual house, and as holy priests, we can offer spiritual sacrifices of praise and worship to God. Revelation 5 tells us that one day the living creatures, elders, angels, creatures in heaven, on the earth and under the earth, and such as are in the sea, and all that is in them will say, "Blessing and honour and glory and power Be to Him who sits on the throne, And to the Lamb, forever and ever!" (see Revelation 5:9-14).

In the meantime, let the living stones cry out in worship!

Day 79

By faith we understand

Now faith is the substance of things hoped for, the evidence of things not seen. For by it the elders obtained a good testimony. By faith we understand that the worlds were framed by the word of God, so that the things which are seen were not made of things which are visible. (Hebrews 11:1-3)

Hebrews 11 is about the reality of faith. It is the confidence and assurance of things looked for in the future. In everyday language, we often use the word "hope" to describe what we want to happen, but cannot be sure it will. On the other hand, hope is always used in the New Testament to mean a future certainty. This hope is described in Hebrews 6:19-20 as being "an anchor of the soul, both sure and steadfast, and which enters the Presence behind the veil, where the forerunner has entered for us, even Jesus, having become High Priest forever according to the order of Melchizedek." Later, John writes that this hope is in the Person of Jesus Christ and it has a purifying effect on our lives: "And everyone who has this hope in Him purifies himself, just as He is pure" (1 John 3:3). Faith in God is ancient and has worked effectively in the lives of the people of God from their beginning; by it we understand creation and we know the invisible God.

When I was at school, I developed an interest in art, which was fostered by my art teacher. One day he arranged to take our class to the local art gallery. It was a visit I have always remembered. We went from room to room, looking at the great pictures hanging from the high walls. Each one told its own story. The longer you looked at a work of art, the more you discovered about what the artist had painted. In Hebrews 11 we are taken into God's picture gallery of faith. We are invited to look back at the lives of great men and women of God. The longer we look, the more we discover about the remarkable power of faith displayed in their lives. Their faith is all the more remarkable because they did not have the completed Scriptures as we do. They had no knowledge of a risen, glorified Christ as we have. They had not experienced the Holy Spirit's permanent and abiding presence as the Church has since Pentecost. But their remarkable lives teach us what it means to simply trust God.

The characters listed in the chapter were not without their faults. They made many mistakes and sometimes big ones. But when their lives are recorded in this chapter, we see only their faith. I remember the words of a dear Christian who, when he was in his nineties, told me that Hebrews 11 is not about the failures of God's people but the faith of God's people. This teaches us something important about how God looks upon His people. He sees us through Christ. Our Father rejoices in His children's faith, and He deals quietly with our failures. This encourages us to rejoice in the faith of our fellow Christians, rather than dwelling, as we sometimes do, on their failures.

It seems to me that God was not only saying these people had faith, but in each of their stories the power of faith was demonstrated in an important and distinctive way. As we consider how they trusted in God and how He responded to their faith, we are encouraged to trust God in a more direct and straightforward way amidst the unbelief that surrounds us in today's world. It is a journey on which we discover "the victory that has overcome the world – our faith" (1 John 5:4).

Day 80

Faith to approach God

---

*By faith Abel offered to God a more excellent sacrifice than Cain,
through which he obtained witness that he was righteous, God
testifying of his gifts; and through it he being dead still speaks*

(Hebrews 11:4)

The story of faith begins with Abel. He and his brother Cain
had never had the fellowship with God that their father and
mother had known. Abel is the first man referred to as "a keeper
of sheep" – a shepherd – in Genesis 4:2. His brother Cain was
a farmer. These two brothers represent two themes which run
through the whole Bible: the spiritual man and the natural man.
Cain is an extreme illustration of the natural man, filled with
envy, rage, violence and deceit. Cain has no place in Hebrews
11, but Abel, the first man of faith and the first martyr, does
have.

Faith begins by approaching God on the basis of sacrifice
and the need for salvation. In the lamb Abel sacrificed as his
substitute, God reminds us of the Lamb of God who takes
away the sin of the world. Abel reminds us of a sinner, in need
of salvation, expressing faith in a sinless sacrifice, the Lamb of
God. He later reminds us of a Saviour, a Shepherd that died at
the hands of wicked men. It always amazes me how God takes
every opportunity to embed within His word the Person and
work of His beloved Son. He did this before sin entered the
world, when He caused Adam to fall into a deep sleep so that
God could take a rib and form Eve, a beautiful picture of Christ
loving the Church and giving Himself for her. God also did

this when He made the first sacrifice to clothe Adam and Eve (Genesis 3:21).

Cain and Abel present two different approaches to God. Cain approached God with the fruit of the land he farmed. He came to God offering the efforts of his own labour – good works. Abel learned, by direct revelation or from his parents, that the way to God was through the sacrifice of a life. Abel's sacrifice, as we have said, looked on to the time when Christ Himself would come into the world as the Saviour and sacrifice Himself upon the cross. Christ took our place and died in our stead. He was the great substitute and the only way to God: "I am the way, the truth, and the life. No one comes to the Father except through me" (John 14:6). We approach God in this way for salvation and enjoy the fullness of His salvation. The Christ who died for us now lives for us in heaven: "He is also able to save to the uttermost those who come to God through Him, since He always lives to make intercession for them" (Hebrews 7:25).

The story of faith begins by introducing us to the all-sufficiency of Christ represented in a tiny lamb. Through Abel's faith and obedience, he was made righteous. First of all, faith teaches us salvation and righteousness are in Christ. All the sacrifices of the Old Testament looked forward to the one great sacrifice Christ would make: "But this Man, after He had offered one sacrifice for sins forever, sat down at the right hand of God" (Hebrews 10:12). The life of faith begins at the foot of the cross. It grows in relation to the place the Saviour occupies in our hearts.

Secondly, faith is stimulated by His love and grace. By abiding in Christ by faith, we shall in the words of Psalm 1:3 be

> … like a tree
> Planted by the rivers of water,
> That brings forth its fruit in its season,
> Whose leaf also shall not wither;
> And whatever he does shall prosper.

Day 81

Faith to please God

By faith Enoch was taken away so that he did not see death, "and was not found, because God had taken him"; for before he was taken he had this testimony, that he pleased God. But without faith it is impossible to please Him, for he who comes to God must believe that He is, and that He is a rewarder of those who diligently seek Him.   *(Hebrews 11:5-6)*

Enoch had the faith to please God. He was remarkable for two reasons: first, he walked with (pleased) God (Genesis 5:24), and second, he did not die.

When Jesus was baptised in the River Jordan, the Holy Spirit descended from heaven in the form of a dove, and the Father's voice was heard from heaven, "This is My beloved Son, in whom I am well pleased" (Matthew 3:17). At a conference some years ago, I raised the question, "If heaven opened over my head, what would God say?" I think I would be concerned about all my failures and how little I have pleased God. But God does not want us to become self-occupied. His grace deals with our failings. What is amazing is that we have the potential to please God. Our Heavenly Father is not only expecting us to "bear fruit", "more fruit" and "much fruit" (John 15), He is actively involved in this process in our lives: "I am the true vine, and My Father is the vinedresser. Every branch in Me that does not bear fruit He takes away; and every branch that bears fruit He prunes, that it may bear more fruit" (15:1-2). By describing His Father as "the vinedresser", the Lord Jesus brings home to us how closely the Father works in our lives to make us into the people He wants us, His children, to be.

The Apostle writes, "But without faith it is impossible to please Him, for he who comes to God must believe that He is, and that He is a rewarder of those who diligently seek Him." So what does a life well-pleasing to God look like? Interestingly the detail of Enoch's life is not given to us. But the details of the life of Christ and of so many of the lives of Old and New Testament saints are given to us. We learn from the Person of Christ and the faith of His people. The characteristics and the development of the fruit of the Spirit are also explained to us. What we need is the faith to cultivate the practice of walking humbly with our God (Micah 6:8) in our circumstances and generation.

It has been said that Enoch enjoyed such a close relationship with God that one day God said to Enoch, "Instead of going home, come to My house", and He took him home to heaven. It is an excellent way to think of how Enoch, the first man to be raptured, entered heaven without dying. There is a day coming when the whole Church of Christ will be raptured and taken into the Father's house (1 Thessalonians 4). Until then, we are to live in daily communion with God the Father and God the Son by the power and liberty of God the Holy Spirit, and be guided by the Word of God. In these ways, the love of God empowers us to live by faith. The hope we have in Christ has a purifying effect on our lives. Enoch lived in daily communion with God. He helps to illustrate how the power to please God comes from abiding in Christ day by day, and the God of peace makes us "complete in every good work to do His will, working in you what is well pleasing in His sight, through Jesus Christ, to whom be glory forever and ever. Amen" (Hebrews 13:20-21).

Day 82

Faith to serve God

---

*By faith Noah, being divinely warned of things not yet seen,
moved with godly fear, prepared an ark for the saving of his
household, by which he condemned the world and became heir of
the righteousness which is according to faith.*   *(Hebrews 11:7)*

Noah's story begins with him finding grace in the eyes of
the Lord (Genesis 6:8). Like Abel and Enoch, he lived in an
increasingly violent and corrupt world. But God drew Noah to
Himself, and the thin line of faith continued in this man who
learned to walk with God. After God shared his purposes with
Noah, he gave him a precise service: to build an ark.

In the course of my work I have regular contact with a local
boatyard. I really enjoy going into the big shed where old boats
are restored and new ones built. I always wonder how the
craftsmen begin the work. I never cease to be impressed by the
variety of skills used and the incredible results of painstaking
and detailed work. To see these boats in full sail, cutting through
the waters of the Humber Estuary, is a lovely sight. As people
watch these boats, I doubt many think about the skill, hard
work and devotion that went into creating such remarkable
vessels. So it was with Noah. His ark must have been a mystery
to the people who watched it gradually emerge. The Lord Jesus
reminds us, "As in the days before the flood, they were eating
and drinking, marrying and giving in marriage until the day
that Noah entered the ark" (Matthew 24:38). COVID-19 has
demonstrated how fragile and uncertain life can be. Tragic
circumstances can focus our hearts and minds on the meaning
and purpose of life. They can draw us near to God, but they can

also cause us to resist God or, as in Noah's day, simply not to care. The Lord experienced what is was for no one to care for his soul (Psalm 142:4), but it is a solemn and tragic thing when we don't care for our own souls.

As the world continued in its distance from God, Noah continued in his nearness to God. The world did not mould him into its character. He was transformed through faith. And how was this seen? It was seen in his personal walk with God, care for his family, the witness of his work, and by preaching righteousness (2 Peter 2:5). This is also our witness. We should not forget that Noah saved his family. It is a challenge to Christians that, in our endeavour to serve others, our families are not neglected. Noah kept his varied responsibilities in balance, and his life was a harmonious witness to the grace of God in the world he lived in.

Service can sometimes feel a fruitless occupation. It can seem that no one listens or understands. The Lord Jesus had the experience of seeing little response to His own ministry at times. But God does not assess our lives based on the degree of our success, but upon our willingness to be faithful servants. Today endless attempts are made to try to measure levels of success in education, business and society. The results are always imperfect. But God knows the effort, tears, disappointments and trials we go through in trying to serve Him. He values perfectly what we do for Him, and He uses our service in ways which are only known to Him. Finally, He delights to say, "Well done, good and faithful servant; you were faithful over a few things, I will make you ruler over many things. Enter into the joy of your lord" (Matthew 25:21).

Day 83

Faith to obey and to receive

By faith Abraham obeyed when he was called to go out to the place which he would receive as an inheritance. And he went out, not knowing where he was going. (Hebrews 11:8)

By faith Sarah herself also received strength to conceive seed, and she bore a child when she was past the age, because she judged Him faithful who had promised. (Hebrews 11:11)

There is one person who is mentioned concerning the power of faith more than any other – Abraham. In verse 8 we are told Abraham had the faith to obey God. He simply believed God and was willing to start out on a path, not knowing where it would lead him. All great men and women of faith have been able to trust God in this way. As an uneducated young Christian, Gladys Aylward was employed as a cleaner. She was convinced that God was calling her to serve Him in China. She approached the China Inland Mission, but was rejected. Undaunted, she saved every week until she had the fare to take the daunting Trans-Siberian rail journey alone to China. Her astonishing story is told in the book "The London Sparrow". We are not all called to China, but we are called to obey God. Obedience is something all Christians struggle with, and its simplicity confounds us. But on those rare occasions when, by one circumstance or another, we are forced to have complete faith in God, we discover the joy of knowing that God really does respond to our trust in Him.

Like Noah, Abraham's faith was shared by his wife, Sarah (v. 11). If you read Sarah's story in Genesis 18, you will learn that she laughed at the news that she would become a mother in her old age. Hardly an act of faith, you would think. But later, when Isaac, whose name means "he laughs", is born, Sarah says, "God has made me laugh, and all who hear will laugh with me." This was the joy of faith. Sarah understood the work of God in her life and the fulfilment of God's promises to Abraham in Isaac. She had the faith to receive from God and rejoice in what He accomplished in her life.

This is an essential aspect of faith. We need to have the faith to receive from God. In Malachi 3, God says to His people:

> "Try Me now in this …
> If I will not open for you the windows of heaven
> And pour out for you such blessing
> That there will not be room enough to receive it."

In 2 Kings 4, when Elisha asks the widow who was in debt what she has in the house, she had nothing but a jar of oil. He tells her to borrow vessels from everywhere and to fill them with the oil from the jar. She had the faith to receive, and found as many containers as she could. She did not run out of oil; she ran out of containers to fill! Only then did the flow of oil stop. She had faith to receive. We need to ask God to enable us to receive the blessing He wants to give us through faith: only believe.

It is always encouraging to see faith expressed in a married couple, like Abraham and Sarah. It is so important to uphold before the throne of grace our Christian marriages. Faith is needed not only for our personal walk with God, but also as we walk in love together for the glory of God.

Day 84

Faith to sacrifice

By faith Abraham, when he was tested, offered up Isaac, and he who had received the promises offered up his only begotten son, of whom it was said, "In Isaac your seed shall be called," concluding that God was able to raise him up, even from the dead, from which he also received him in a figurative sense. By faith Isaac blessed Jacob and Esau concerning things to come.

(Hebrews 11:17-20)

Abraham did not know where he was going when God first tested his faith. But verse 2 of Genesis 22 recalls the occasion when God told Abraham exactly where to go and what to do. Abraham had to go to the land of Moriah and sacrifice Isaac on one of the mountains there. It was the greatest test of Abraham's remarkable faith.

We are shocked that God would ask Abraham to do such a thing. And what possible purpose did God have, given that Isaac was Abraham's heir and the embodiment of all the promises God had made to the patriarch?

But Abraham doesn't question God's command. Abraham was very good at appealing to God. For example, he pleaded to God to spare Sodom. Abraham prayed for God to accept Ishmael to be his heir before Isaac was born. He wasn't afraid to ask God to change His decisions. But this time, instead of trying to alter the situation, Abraham immediately responds to God's command and sets out for the land of Moriah. He had learned to completely trust in His God. He had the faith to sacrifice to God and concluded that God was able to raise up Isaac from the dead, which is what happened in a figurative sense. Isaac's faith was also remarkable. He never resisted the circumstances he found himself in, but willingly and calmly submitted to them.

In the first book in the Bible, God teaches us, through Abraham's faith, about the sacrifice He himself would make in the gift of His only Son, Jesus Christ, whom He loved. God foretold, in the faith of Isaac, the time when Jesus, in response to the Father's will and in love for us, would become the sacrifice for the sin of the world (John 3:16) and that He would rise again (Hebrews 13:20).

The story teaches us several important things about faith:

- True faith rests entirely upon God;

- God sometimes tests our faith to sacrifice, without requiring us to do so, but to strengthen our faith in Him;

- Complete belief in God's will and purposes and a willingness to live a sacrificial life of service are at the centre of the life of faith.

God's whole relationship with us is based on a love that sacrifices. That love produces a sacrificial response from our lives: "Therefore by Him let us continually offer the sacrifice of praise to God, that is, the fruit of our lips, giving thanks to His name. But do not forget to do good and to share, for with such sacrifices God is well pleased" (Hebrews 13:15-16).

Day 85

The fire of the Lord and rain of the Lord

Then the fire of the LORD fell and consumed the burnt sacrifice, and the wood and the stones and the dust, and it licked up the water that was in the trench. Now when all the people saw it, they fell on their faces; and they said, "The LORD, He is God! The LORD, He is God!" (1 Kings 18:38-39)

The sound of abundance of rain. (1 Kings 18:41)

In 1 Kings 18 we read the remarkable account of how, under the hand of God, the prophet Elijah speaks to the heart of the nation of Israel at Mount Carmel. At the time of the offering of the evening sacrifice (v. 36), Elijah prayed to God. All the sacrifices instituted by God in the Old Testament looked on to the one perfect sacrifice revealed in the New Testament: the sacrifice of the Lord Jesus as the Lamb of God. All God's love and blessing are demonstrated through His sacrifice. God the Father gave the Son, and the Son of God gave Himself. We have life because the Lord Jesus sacrificed Himself for us. Elijah prayed to the living God, the God of Abraham, Isaac and Jacob (Matthew 22:32). He simply asks, "Hear me, O Lord, hear me, that this people may know that You are the Lord God, and that You have turned their hearts back to You again" (v. 37). His prayer is based on Who God is.

God's response to his prayer was as instantaneous as it was powerful. That it happened so quickly and so powerfully shows how much God wanted His people to know Him. The power of the fire from heaven was astounding and consumed the sacrifice, wood, stones, dust and water. But it was also controlled. The world has seen great fires but none so powerful, so focussed and controlled as this. Neither Elijah, the people or even the prophets of Baal were harmed by it. Yet it consumed the sacrifice and everything associated with it. At Calvary, the power of God's judgement and love are seen. At the cross, the Lord Jesus bore in His own body our sins. God's judgement fell in all its terror, holiness and sheer power upon His Son, Jesus. God's judgement did not fall on the Jews in their rejection and hatred, or the Romans in their injustice and arrogance. It did not fall on the indifferent passers-by or the sorrowing disciples or the dying thieves close by. It fell wholly and entirely on our Saviour.

What came from heaven next in 1 Kings 17 was "the sound of abundance of rain". The fire of judgement which came from heaven was followed by the extraordinary abundance and blessing of rain from heaven. Life was given where, during the drought, death had reigned.

My father did his national service in Palestine and was stationed at Haifa, below Mount Carmel. Many years later, I stood on Mount Carmel, looking out over the Mediterranean Sea, thinking of the day Elijah saw the rain coming. He saw in type what we enjoy in reality: the windows of heaven opened, and every spiritual blessing in Christ Jesus (Ephesians 1:3) poured out upon us. And why? It's because the Son of God loved me and gave Himself for me. God's heart overflows in blessing to us. The joy of worship is that our hearts burst in praise and gratitude to the Saviour whose endless love rests on us.

Day 86

Faith to bless and faith to worship

*By faith Jacob, when he was dying, blessed each of the sons of
Joseph, and worshipped, leaning on the top of his staff.*

(Hebrews 11:21)

The faith to bless is mentioned concerning both Isaac and Jacob
in verses 20 and 21. This is a beautiful aspect of the power of
faith. It is one thing to be blessed and another to be a blessing.
Jacob, as a young man, wanted to be blessed. He tricked his
older brother out of his birthright and was encouraged by his
mother to deceive Isaac into blessing him above Esau. As a
result, he had to flee from his home in fear of Esau. That night,
as he slept at Bethel, God appeared to him in a remarkable
dream and promised to be with Jacob and bring him safely
home. Jacob spent the next twenty difficult years in the house
of Laban before making the return journey. The night before
he met Esau, he again found himself alone with God at Penuel.
And he wrestled with the Angel of God, eventually pleading
with God to bless him. God gave him a new name, Israel, and
blessed him. Jacob had the faith to ask God to bless him, and
for the rest of his life he became a blessing to others. He blessed
Esau; he blessed Pharaoh; he blessed his sons; and he blessed
his grandchildren. His life was transformed from selfishness to
selflessness.

God blesses us and He wants to make us a blessing to others. I
once found myself in the middle of the Sea of Galilee in a boat
with a group of Roman Catholics who had kindly let me share
their trip. Before we returned to shore, the priest spoke about
the River Jordan. He explained that the river flowed into the Sea

of Galilee and finally down to the Dead Sea. He compared the Sea of Galilee and its fertile surroundings to being blessed and allowing that blessing to flow out. But, he said, the flowing of the Jordan stopped at the Dead Sea. Then he asked us a simple question, "What kind of Christians are we? Does blessing flow from us or simply stop with us?" I have never forgotten his short word of ministry. God blesses us through faith, and we need faith to be a blessing to others. Think of the experiences we have of God's goodness. Think about how we have the opportunity to pass on the blessing of God to others by sharing the Gospel, and through words and actions of kindness, sympathy and care.

Jacob had faith to bless others and faith to worship (v. 21). We are not only called to bless our fellow believers and neighbours, but we are called to be worshippers. Jesus explained to the woman at Sychar's well in John 4 that the Father is seeking worshippers (v. 23). We might have thought of Enoch, Noah, Abraham and Isaac as great worshippers – and, of course, they were. But God chooses Jacob, the transformed man, who could speak of God as the "God who shepherded me all the days of my life" (Genesis 48:15), as a worshipper. Jacob who, as a young man, so misunderstood the character of God, in later years had such a profound understanding of His grace. After the experience at Peniel ("the face of God"), Jacob limped. This was a constant reminder of the day he met God, and God blessing him. He became the man who built altars to worship God and who ended his days as a worshipper. True men and woman of faith are true worshippers. If we do not make time to worship God, we can never truly serve Him. Serving God is, of course, so important, but it begins with us coming into His presence in faith to worship Him.

Day 87

Tuesday

Faith to hope

By faith Joseph, when he was dying, made mention of the departure of the children of Israel, and gave instructions concerning his bones. (Hebrews 11:22)

Joseph is one of the most remarkable men in the Bible. Like the Lord Jesus, he was loved by his father and hated by his brothers. He suffered at the hands of his brothers and they sold him into slavery. He endured injustice and imprisonment. But in a marvellous illustration of resurrection, he emerges from prison to become a saviour. God was with Joseph. He protected him from his brothers, in Potiphar's house and in prison. God blessed Him in everything he did. Joseph came out of jail, not only to interpret Pharaoh's dream but to transform his kingdom. He was a man who by God's grace developed the greatest nation on earth at that time. And, in saving the kingdom from famine, Joseph, in fulfilment of God's will, was able to save his own family and once more see his father who loved him so dearly. He did all of this by God's hand. You would think there were so many things Joseph achieved which could have been recorded in Hebrews to describe his faith.

The most surprising is the one that we read about: the instructions he gave concerning his bones (Genesis 50:25). You would be forgiven for asking why this was so important. It was important because it shows us that Joseph looked to the future; he had hope. Although he lived such a powerful life in Egypt, his heart was in the Promised Land. Joseph had faith to look forward to the time when his people would leave Egypt and inherit the land God gave them. He believed in the promises of God. And, sure enough, when Moses left Egypt on the Passover night, he took the body of Joseph with him. It has been said that Joseph had the longest funeral in history. It lasted over forty years! As the children of Israel travelled through the wilderness, Joseph went everywhere with them. Until at last, Joshua took the people into the Promised Land, and Joseph, the great man of God, was buried at Shechem (Joshua 24:32). He is a reminder of the Lord Jesus. At the end of the book of Genesis, Joseph is the promise of hope. At the end of the book of Joshua, he is the fulfilment of hope.

Christianity is characterised by three things: Faith, Hope and Love. The greatest of these is Love, which is eternal. Faith will give way to sight, and Hope will be fulfilled. But now we have a living faith and a living hope. The hope of the Christian in the Bible refers to something future, but absolutely sure. Joseph believed with full certainty that God would lead His people to the Promised Land, and he prepared for that event. We believe that one day Christ is coming again, and, in the words of the Apostle Paul, "we shall always be with the Lord" (1 Thessalonians 4:17). In the words of John, "we shall be like Him, for we shall see Him as He is" (1 John 3:2). This is a purifying hope: "And everyone who has this hope in Him purifies himself, just as He is pure" (1 John 3:3). And, of course, the Lord Jesus said, "I will come again and receive you to Myself" (John 14:3). The challenge of faith is to live in the light of the reality of Christ's coming. This hope transformed the lives of early Christians. Their watchword was, "Maranatha" ("Our Lord, come!"). Waiting for the Lord stirs us to service. Watching for the Lord stirs us to worship.

Day 88

I have learned

Everywhere and in all things I have learned both to be full and to be hungry, both to abound and to suffer need. I can do all things through Christ who strengthens me. (Philippians 4:12-13)

Paul spends most of the final part of the last chapter of Philippians teaching us about learning. He begins (v. 8) by explaining that learning starts with observation and meditation. Paul asks his brethren to observe the things that are true, honourable, just, pure, lovely and commendable. So often the vast range of the communication systems of the world can be occupied with what is untrue, dishonourable, unjust, impure, ugly and unworthy. We enrich or endanger our minds by what we allow them to focus on. The features Paul describes are features which should mark every Christian. They are positive and valuable characteristics. We find them displayed in the Old Testament saints and perfectly expressed in the life of Christ. We learn from them by observing them, carefully considering them and replicating them in our own lives by the power of the Holy Spirit. The Philippians had seen these characteristics in Paul, and he encourages them to follow his example. As he followed the Lord, he experienced the presence of the God of peace, and he assured his readers of the same experience.

There is a feature of Paul's ministry which is very appealing. Even when he is speaking to mature Christians, he teaches them things they knew well as though he was teaching them for the first time. This brings a freshness and vitality to his ministry. We should never lose the wonder of the things of God, whether new or old. The things of God should never be commonplace, but always fill us with joy and hope in believing, and encourage us to continue to fulfil God's will in our lives.

Paul rejoices in the evidence of the Philippians' care for him. It demonstrated that his teaching had already borne fruit in their lives. He was full of gratitude for their repeated care towards him: "But I rejoiced in the Lord greatly that now at last your care for me has flourished again."

Paul used the Philippians' care towards him as an opportunity to teach them about his own learning: "I have learned in whatever state I am, to be content." The Apostle had "learned the secret of facing plenty and hunger, abundance and need (v. 12, ESV). When we are in need, it casts us on the Lord, and we draw close to Him. But what about when we are full and abound? Are we less dependent and become more self-confident and self-reliant? And, as a consequence, more distant from the Lord? Paul brings everything into focus when he writes, "I can do all things through Christ who strengthens me." Needs and circumstances change. But whatever those circumstances are – pleasant or testing – we need the presence and power of the Saviour.

In chapter 1 Paul wrote that he had the Philippian saints in his heart. But since he knew what it was to be forsaken and forgotten in his service for God, it must have been such a joy to him to know he was in the hearts of the Philippians. Their gift was not of primary importance, but the love that sent it was: "You shared in my distress." He rejoices in their sacrificial giving as evidence of how those dear people of God had so learned Christ. He assures them, and us, that "My God shall supply all your need according to His riches in glory by Christ Jesus" and bowed his heart in worship: "Now to our God and Father be glory forever and ever. Amen."

Day 89

Our God will be our guide

Great is the LORD, and greatly to be praised...
... that you may tell the next generation
that this is God,
our God forever and ever.
He will guide us beyond death.

(Psalm 48:1 and 13-14, ESV margin)

The famous comedian Groucho Marx was once at a dinner party when the conversation turned to marriage. One of the guests asked him, "How long have you been married, Groucho?" The comedian replied, "I have been married forty years, and it just seems like yesterday." Then he added, "And you know what a bad day yesterday was!"

On 26th September, 1970 something very special happened: I was married to my wife June. If you asked me today, "How long have you been married, Gordon?" I would reply, "I have been married fifty years, and it just seems like yesterday." Then I would add, "And you know what a good day yesterday was!"

I don't say this because our marriage has been a continuously smooth and calm experience. Marriage is a mixture of joys and sorrows, along with the immense pleasure of loving and being loved through many crises, sorrows, disagreements and mistakes. No, the wonder of Christian marriage is the constant and mutual discovery that "Great is the Lord, and greatly to be praised." From the very beginning, it was in God's mind that men and women would reflect the love of God in their relationship. Within their marriages, He wanted them to express His love. This love would be shown to one another, to their children, to their families and to their neighbours. Their lives were to be an outflowing of the blessing of God, lives that would exclaim, "Great is the Lord, and greatly to be praised."

When we were engaged, June bought me a watch and on the wrist strap was engraved Psalm 48:14 (KJV), "For this God is our God for ever and ever: he will be our guide even unto death." It was in anticipation of our marriage vows, "till death us do part". I like the ESV translation and *margin*:

> that you may tell the next generation
> that this is God,
> our God forever and ever.
> *He will guide us beyond death.*

The writer is talking about telling the next generation. Our marriages are a witness to the love of Christ to both the present and next generations. In Christian marriage we should have the experience of knowing God as our God in shared faith and love. He wants us to know His presence in our marriages. This presence guides us throughout our lives together. But more than this, we have a shared hope. His love guides us beyond death.

There is intended in Christian marriage a reflection of Christ's sacrificial love for the Church: "Husbands, love your wives, just as Christ also loved the church and gave Himself for her" (Ephesians 5:25). Paul speaks about the Church in all her future glory: a glorious Church (v. 27). God's love welcomes us within its eternal embrace because Christ's love has conquered death. Like David, the great Psalmist, we can all join our hearts and voices together today and, looking forward, say, "Surely goodness and mercy shall follow us all the days of our lives; and we will dwell in the house of the Lord forever (see Psalm 23:6). May God bless and keep us in our marriages.

Day 90

Miletus

From Miletus he sent to Ephesus and called for the elders of the church. And when they had come to him, he said to them: "You know, from the first day that I came to Asia, in what manner I always lived among you, serving the Lord with all humility, with many tears and trials." (Acts 20:17-19)

Paul's meeting with the Ephesian elders on his journey to Jerusalem gives us a great insight into the characteristics of faithful service to God. Paul was about to enter into a phase of his ministry which would be the culmination of the Lord's words in Acts 9:15-16: "He is a chosen vessel of Mine to bear My name before Gentiles, kings, and the children of Israel. For I will show him how many things he must suffer for My name's sake." Paul knew he had to return in faith to Jerusalem. It was the path that would lead to Rome. The Holy Spirit had foretold that imprisonment and suffering lay before him. But Paul was prepared to risk his life fulfilling the ministry he had received from his Saviour. He wasn't going to finish it in fear, but in joyful faith. At Miletus he took the opportunity to exhort the Ephesian elders to care spiritually for the flock of God at Ephesus. He did this by giving them the example of his own service.

Paul was marked in this service by consistency ("from the first day") and humility ("serving the Lord with all humility") in the face of considerable opposition ("many tears and trials"). He had "kept nothing back" (v. 20), but faithfully, extensively and systematically taught the people of God publicly and in their homes. At the same time he was preaching the Gospel to all men, appealing for "repentance toward God and faith toward our Lord Jesus Christ". This testimony of his compassion in the Gospel and declaration of the whole counsel of God had been completed in Ephesus in terms of his physical presence. And he spoke directly to the elders about their responsibility to care spiritually for themselves so that they could shepherd all the flock under the direction of the Holy Spirit. He impresses upon them what God had impressed indelibly upon his own heart: the preciousness of the Church and the cost of her redemption, the blood of Christ, the Son of God. He was once a savage wolf but became a tender – and like David – a fearless shepherd. Paul saw the dangers to the flock because he had once been a danger to it. And with a shepherd's heart he strove to prepare them for external and internal attacks upon their faith and confidence in Christ. Paul commends them to God and to the word of His grace. He had left them an example of a selfless life which sought no material gain. He had willingly worked in a practical way to provide for himself and his fellow workers, so fulfilling the law of Christ – love. Finally, he turns their hearts to the Lord Jesus and kneels down to lift them up before the Throne of God.

At Miletus, through his servant Paul, the Lord Jesus encourages us to serve Him with full hearts, faithfully, humbly, compassionately, and consistently. He teaches us to ensure we live close to the Saviour so that we can care for each other and share the Gospel. We are to be aware of, and prepared for, attacks on our faith. We need to be confident in the God of all grace and led by the light of the word of His grace; praying without ceasing; walking in faith the pathway He lays out before us. Miletus is an object lesson in faithful service to God that we should not ignore.

Day 91

Not forgotten

I commend to you Phoebe our sister ... and Quartus a brother

(Romans 16:1 and 23)

I have always found the first and last words and chapters of the books of the Bible particularly interesting. Having said that, you might be forgiven for thinking that Romans 16 is mostly a list of the names of Paul's friends, with little relevance today. God has written lists of the names of lots of people in the Bible. Most of them we know nothing about. But God knows everything about them. Unless we are particularly famous, our names will be forgotten by people relatively quickly. The pressures of modern life, and certainly the increasing restrictions of the COVID crisis, can make many of us feel lonely and isolated. But God's value of us is immense and we have a Saviour who tells us our names are on His shoulders, on His heart (see Exodus 28:12, 29) and on the palms of His hands:

> "I will not forget you.
> Behold, I have engraved you on the palms of my
> hands" (Isaiah 49:15-16).

Paul gives us a sense of this value as he remembers his friends and fellow believers. He recalls many people by name and refers to others. These include ten women: Phoebe, Priscilla, Mary, Tryphena and Tryphosa, Persis, Rufus' mother, Nereus' sister, Junia and Julia. Phoebe is mentioned first as a servant of the church and helper of many. That is such a simple but powerful description: the Holy Spirit is called *the* Helper. Paul remembers Andronicus and Junia, who may have been husband and wife. They were his kinsmen (ESV) and fellow prisoners, well respected by the apostles and had been Christians for about twenty-five years. Paul highlights the features we should value as the people of God: lives of service, strong Christian relationships, suffering, experience, generosity and learning. We should never let the frailty and weakness of older Christians cause us to forget the value of lifelong discipleship lived for God.

At the same time, younger people were also in Paul's heart and mind. Timothy is an outstanding example of this in verse 21. The Christian homes and families of Priscilla and Aquila (v. 3), Aristobulus (v. 10), Narcissus (v. 11) and Gaius (v. 23) are highlighted. Family homes were places of hospitality and often where churches met. The Christian home was central to the early Christian church. Today, against a background of widespread family breakdown, our homes are at the forefront of the Christian testimony. The greater and the less are placed together in verse 23: "Erastus, the city treasurer, and our brother Quartus, greet you" (ESV). The early church was not a place where partiality was permitted, but the distinguished and the ordinary were equal in the sight of God.

Paul ends his great letter with the God of peace and grace (20), power (25), and wisdom and glory (27). We know the God of peace and the grace of our Lord Jesus Christ. We have the all-powerful Spirit of God dwelling within our hearts. The wisdom of God is revealed to us in His word, and in Christ we have the hope of glory. He has not, nor will he ever, forget any of His people:

> For He is our God,
> And we are the people of His pasture,
> And the sheep of His hand (Psalm 95:7).

Day 92

Bethany

Then, six days before the Passover, Jesus came to Bethany, where Lazarus was who had been dead, whom He had raised from the dead. There they made Him a supper, and Martha served, but Lazarus was one of those who sat at the table with Him. Then Mary took a pound of very costly oil of spikenard, anointed the feet of Jesus, and wiped His feet with her hair. And the house was filled with the fragrance of the oil. (John 12:1-3)

Bethany was the place where Jesus said to Martha, "I am the resurrection and the life." It was the place where He demonstrated the reality of what He had said when He raised Lazarus to life in the most remarkable of all His miracles. And it was also the place where Martha declared, "Yes, Lord, I believe that You are the Christ, the Son of God, who is to come into the world" (John 11:25, 27). At the beginning of chapter 12 Jesus returns to Bethany. The Passover was only six days away.

We read in John 19 the account of how, on the Preparation Day of the Passover, Pilate spoke to the representatives of the nation of Israel about Jesus: "Behold, I am bringing Him out to you, that you may know that I find no fault in Him." He brought Jesus out, wearing the crown of thorns and the purple robe, and said, "Behold the Man!" (John 19:4-5). The hate-filled and deafening response was, "Crucify Him, crucify Him!" A little later Pilate said to them, "Behold your King!" (John 19:14) and again the people cried out, "Away with Him, away with Him! Crucify Him!" Pilate asked them, "Shall I crucify your King?" and the chief priests answered, "We have no king but Caesar!" Jesus was then delivered to them to be crucified.

As all this awaited the Lord, He went to Bethany, the home of those He loved: "Jesus loved Martha and her sister and Lazarus" (John 11:5). And we are told they made Him a supper. They expressed their love and gratitude for the Lord in a meal in His honour. I don't think we always understand what it meant to the Lord to be received in this simple way. In the glorious beginning of John's Gospel we learn of the deity of the Person of Christ. And soon afterwards we read about the rejection He faced by His own people. As John writes, "But as many as received Him, to them He gave the right to become children of God, to those who believe in His name: who were born, not of blood, nor of the will of the flesh, nor of the will of man, but of God (John 1:12-13). At Bethany the Lord had fellowship with Lazarus, He was served by Martha, and He was worshipped by Mary. The Lord was received by this tiny group of people. The Person, who is the centre of eternity, was the centre of their hearts.

When the Lord stood and heard His people's hatred of Him, His heart was broken by their reproach. But when we gather around Him in fellowship, when we seek to faithfully serve Him, and when we pour out the worship of our hearts to Him, His heart is filled with joy. The Lord wanted to be in Bethany, and He wanted to be in the upper room with His disciples to celebrate the Passover and institute a simple supper that would forever remind us of His suffering love. And He promises to be with us as we remember and respond to His love.

Day 93

Losing donkeys and keeping sheep

Now the donkeys of Kish, Saul's father, were lost. And Kish said to his son Saul, "Please take one of the servants with you, and arise, go and look for the donkeys." (1 Samuel 9:3)

And Samuel said to Jesse, "Are all the young men here?" Then he said, "There remains yet the youngest, and there he is, keeping the sheep." And Samuel said to Jesse, "Send and bring him."

(1 Samuel 16:11)

Samuel was Israel's most outstanding judge. But as his ministry drew to a close, Samuel appointed his sons as judges. It must have been heartbreaking for Samuel to discover his sons did not follow in his ways, but used their privileged positions to financially profit themselves and pervert the course of justice. It is striking that God judged Eli for the failure of his house, but God did not judge Samuel. God is the true judge of how we bring up our children. Ultimately they become responsible to God for the path they take in life. The failure of Samuel's sons influenced Israel to ask for a king so that they could be like other nations. It was a national desire which reflected the spiritual condition of the people of God. We are always in danger of dismissing a pattern God has given us because we fail in carrying it out. We need to consider carefully what we are really discarding. The people's decision was not a rejection of Samuel or even his sons, but the rejection of God Himself. Change can be exciting and full of promise, but a real change has to begin in our hearts.

God gave Israel the kind of king they were looking for: a young, attractive giant of a man. And although Saul started well, his reign ended in disobedience and disaster. In preparation for this, God chose a second man to become king over His people: David. When we are introduced to Saul, he is looking for his father's donkeys that were lost, and which he never found. They were found for him. When we are introduced to David, he is keeping his father's sheep. It was in this lowly occupation of shepherding that David learned to worship and trust God. He didn't lose sheep. David risked his life to protect his father's sheep against a lion and a bear. He fought battles which only God saw. This equipped him to fight and be victorious in the great struggles he would later face. David was a lesson to the nation about what really mattered: a living relationship and implicit trust in the living God. Israel thought that becoming like all other nations would improve their lives. But changing the approach to their government was simply a mask to disguise turning their back on God. What needed changing was hearts that were so far away from God. It is foolishness to blame our failure on people or things. The path of blessing starts at the foot of the cross. There we understand what we are in the flesh and there we know the love which alone can transform us. God bore with Israel and allowed them to reject Him as their King, and discover the consequences. But then, in grace, He gave them a king like no other, one who believed above all else that the Lord was His shepherd – and God made David the shepherd of a nation. Our relationship with Christ changes our relationship with everything. We don't find failure in people and things; we find the power to love and act in grace, and discover the paths He wants us to take to witness to Him.

Day 94

Overcoming temptation

The word of God abides in you,
And you have overcome the wicked one. (1 John 2:14)

There was once a wealthy lady who had a great estate and many servants. Unfortunately the driver of her coach died and she advertised for a replacement driver. Three men were interviewed for the job. During the interviews, she presented the applicants with a problem: "On the approach to my estate the road is very narrow with a steep incline at each side. How near could you drive to the edge of that part of the road without endangering my safety?" The first applicant answered, "I could drive your coach to within one foot of the edge of the road and you would be safe." The second coach driver was even more confident: "I could safely drive to within six inches of the edge of the road." When the last coach driver was presented with the problem, he looked steadfastly at the lady and said, "Madam, I would stay as far from the edge as possible." He got the job!

When we are faced with temptation, what kind of coach driver are we like? Do we go as near to 'the edge' as we can or do we make sure we stay as far away from it as possible? Genesis 3 records the very first temptation. Satan questioned the authority of God: "Has God said?" Then He contradicted the word of God: "You will not surely die." Finally, he promised a lie: "You will be like God." Eve was taken over 'the edge'. Temptation affects our body (food), soul (pleasant) and spirit (wisdom). If we are defeated by temptation, it robs us of the blessings of God, and the pain it causes is never confined to those who commit it.

Jesus was confronted by Satan at the beginning of His public ministry; not in a beautiful garden but as a lowly, hungry and isolated man in a desolate wilderness (Matthew 4:1-11). Satan tried to take Jesus to the edge by challenging His Person: "If you are the Son of God…" He pressed Jesus to command stones to become bread to prove who He was. Jesus demonstrated that He is the Son of God by His obedience to "every word of God" (Luke 4:4), not the fulfilment of His immediate physical needs. Satan then tries to take Jesus to the edge, on a pinnacle of the temple, challenging Him to prove He was the Son of God, again using Scripture to support his case. Jesus proves He is the Son of God by His understanding of the true application of God's word: "You shall not tempt the Lord your God." Finally, the devil tries to take Jesus to the edge on the mountain. Satan abandons Scripture and offers Jesus the kingdoms of the world in return for His worship. Jesus proves He is the Son of God by His total faithfulness to God's word and dismisses Satan with the words, "Away with you, Satan! For it is written, 'You shall worship the Lord your God, and Him only you shall serve.'" Jesus conquered the power of Satan at the beginning of His ministry, and in doing so looked on to His complete victory through His death, resurrection and glorious reception into heaven.

We are all subject to temptation, but the Lord teaches us how to have victory over the power of sin and Satan:

> With my whole heart I have sought You;
> Oh, let me not wander from Your commandments!
> Your word I have hidden in my heart,
> That I might not sin against You (Psalm 119:10-11).

Day 95

Dealing with temptation

"How then can I do this great wickedness, and sin against God?"

(Genesis 39:9)

Joseph brothers hated him and as a result he was sold to Midianite traders who took him to Egypt. It is difficult to understand the trauma and distress Joseph endured as he took that journey. The son with the coat of many colours became a slave in Potiphar's house. At the time, Joseph had no understanding of the remarkable way God was going to use his life. Later, he was honoured by Pharaoh and set over all the land of Egypt. His pain was still evident when he married Asenath and called his first son Manasseh: "For God has made me forget all my toil and all my father's house." But in all his sufferings Joseph never lost his faith in God. The reality of that faith is seen in another testing time in his life. God prospered Joseph as a slave. Through his daily faith, industry and attractiveness as a person, he became Potiphar's trusted servant and controlled all that he had. Joseph is an encouragement to us: "And whatever you do in word or deed, do all in the name of the Lord Jesus, giving thanks to God the Father through Him" (Colossians 3:17).

Joseph's remarkable faith was tested through suffering and through temptation. The latter came in the form of Potiphar's wife, who became obsessed with Joseph. God never allows our faith to be tested in order to destroy it. On the contrary, it is tested to prove its strength and genuineness: "In this you greatly rejoice, though now for a little while, if need be, you have been grieved by various trials, that the genuineness of your faith, being much more precious than gold that perishes, though it is tested by fire, may be found to praise, honour, and glory at the revelation of Jesus Christ, whom having not seen you love" (1 Peter 1:6-8).

We often think of Joseph's temptation only in terms of how he eventually ran away from the advances of Potiphar's wife. But that was Joseph's last course of action, not his first. When he was approached by Potiphar's wife, he doesn't run away, but confronts the situation. He is not diminished by his position as a slave or fearful of her power. He had a clear understanding of the consequences of giving way to such a temptation. He explains that he was in a place of trust. To commit adultery with her was wrong and a betrayal of Potiphar's confidence in him. But above all, it was a sin against God. We need the same clarity of thinking when tempted, and to understand the dishonour it brings to our faith in God and the harm it inflicts on ourselves and others.

The temptation persisted, but Joseph stood his ground and avoided the woman's company. Finally, he removed himself from the place of temptation. It was only when he was trapped by circumstances that Joseph's only course of action was to remove himself from harm. Joseph may have been a slave, but by God's grace, he mastered temptation and refused to give way to sin. He rejected temptation for what it is and protected himself and others. In this he was repeatedly resolute. The word of God was hidden in Joseph's heart, and his obedience kept him safe and was used by God to bring him into the most remarkable blessing. May we learn from his example.

Day 96

Burning or burnt out?

They said to each other, "Did not our hearts burn within us while he talked to us on the road, while he opened to us the Scriptures?" And they rose that same hour and returned to Jerusalem.

(Luke 24:32-33)

A bruised reed He will not break,
And smoking flax He will not quench. (Isaiah 42:3)

I have never forgotten a brother telling the story of a local church which caught fire. Everyone in the village helped in trying to put the fire out, and the pastor of the church worked hard passing buckets of water to throw on the fire. As he was doing this, he realised he didn't know the man next to him, who was also helping. The pastor said to the man, "I have never seen you at my church before." The man replied, "Your church has never been on fire before."

After spending time in the Lord's presence listening to Him explaining how the Scriptures always spoke of Him, the two disciples in Luke 24 said that their hearts burned within them. They were filled with an overwhelming sense of the Saviour's presence in love and power. They had very likely seen the Lord Jesus die upon the cross and laid in another man's tomb. All their hopes and expectations were crushed, and they were filled with sadness and confusion. His ministry had set alight their hearts as they followed Him before His death, but the flame had almost gone out. But the resurrected Lord Jesus came alongside them as the great listener, great understander and the great explainer of His sufferings and glory.

The Lord began His ministry using the word of God to defeat Satan. In resurrection, He uses His word to draw His own to Himself, filling them with His presence and dispelling the sadness and dismay in their hearts. The Lord Jesus taught His disciples, and us, a great lesson on that quiet night. He taught us that we find our Saviour in the pages of Holy Scripture. His word brings us into the reality of His presence. Their hearts burned within them before they knew it was the Lord speaking to them. The word was spoken by the One who is the Word. It ignited in them a responsive devotion to Christ and compelled them to share their experience of Him with their fellow disciples and ultimately in witness to the world. Today the Holy Spirit fulfils this same ministry and glorifies Christ in our hearts, empowering us to live for Him.

I can still remember the old grates and coal fires in houses in the 1950s. I used to stay with my grandmother and often sat in front of a dying fire. She could turn over the last smoking ashes, and find embers from which she could begin a blazing new fire. Isaiah writes of this skill, and Jesus recalls it in Matthew 12:20. It is a picture of a candle wick about to go out. Sometimes we feel the weakness which this illustration describes. It is not always a weakness we share with others but bear in our own souls. We can feel burnt out. The Saviour knows how to come close to us when we feel our utter weakness. He can revive the joy and power of our salvation, and restore our souls. It is the Person of the Lord Jesus, revealed to us through the living word of God, who sets our hearts on fire again. The Lord's love can never be extinguished:

> Many waters cannot quench love,
> Nor can the floods drown it (Song of Solomon 8:7).

The love that saved us is the love that keeps us. Christ's love has never stopped burning and He wants it always to burn in our hearts.

Day 97

Friday

Time to climb rooftops

When Jesus saw their faith (Mark 2:5)

A brother was asked to preach the Gospel at a small hall in the absence of the pastor. He was even given a key to open up the room, ready for the small congregation on the Sunday evening. When Sunday evening arrived there was a storm, and the brother was pretty sure no one would turn up. However, he felt responsible and so made the journey. He arrived at the hall soaked to the skin and opened up its doors. As the minutes ticked by, not one person showed up. But just as he got ready to leave, an old lady arrived with a young girl. They smiled and sat down at the front of the hall. The brother started the meeting and preached the Gospel from his heart. Afterwards, he went across to speak to the old lady and discovered she was almost entirely deaf! They said their goodbyes and the brother returned home with a heavy heart. Some days later, the pastor called him and reminded him of his visit. Then he told him that, when the old lady got home, the young girl, her granddaughter, had spent the rest of the evening painstakingly explaining to her grandmother everything the brother had spoken about. That night the old lady, in her mid-eighties, opened her heart to Jesus Christ.

In Mark 2, the house Jesus visited in Capernaum was full to the brim. People could not get near the door as He preached the word to them. Four men arrived carrying their paralysed friend. They found there was no way into the house to see Jesus. True faith overcomes disappointments and challenges, and love finds a way through. I don't know how difficult it was to take a paralysed man onto a rooftop, but that was the easy part. To remove the roof of the house and let their friend down on his bed to the Saviour was the tricky part. But they did it, and we read "When Jesus saw their faith, He said to the paralytic, 'Son, your sins are forgiven you.'"

Some of the scribes had managed to get into the house early to occupy the best seats from which to express criticism of anything Jesus would do. They were astonished at His words, asking, "Who can forgive sins but God alone?" They didn't realise they were in the presence of God. Jesus dismisses their critical minds and, responding to the faith of the man's friends, spoke again to the paralysed man: "I say to you, arise, take up your bed, and go to your house." Immediately he was healed, picked up his bed, and walked into a new life, leaving the onlookers amazed and praising God, for something they had never seen before.

Several years ago in London, some sisters broke through the fencing of a derelict church. Over a period of time, they met inside the church to pray that God would start a work of grace in the building. When I read of this church, it was no longer derelict but had a congregation of around 300 Christians.

As a new week opens out, the Lord encourages us to not to despair when our service appears fruitless, and to carry in prayer those we care for into the presence of the Saviour; to have faith to overcome smallness, storms, deafness, blocked entrances, rooftops and fences; and to expect to see what we have never seen before.

Day 98

Saturday

Guided by the Good, the Great and the Chief Shepherd

The good shepherd gives His life for the sheep.　　　*(John 10:11)*

The God of peace who brought up our Lord Jesus from the dead, that great Shepherd of the sheep.　　　*(Hebrews 13:20)*

And when the Chief Shepherd appears　　　*(1 Peter 5:4)*

Generally, if you see a shepherd in this country, he will be driving his sheep, very often with dogs. But in the Bible, we have brought before us shepherds who led their flocks, guiding them to green pastures and still waters, carrying the young in their arms and fighting off wolves, bears and lions. The whole relationship is closer and very different. It is these shepherds Jesus uses to describe His relationship with His people. In John 10:4 Jesus talks about the shepherd bringing out His own sheep, leading them, and the sheep willingly following the shepherd because they know His voice.

The Good Shepherd: Paul writes in Galatians, "I have been crucified with Christ; it is no longer I who live, but Christ lives in me; and the life which I now live in the flesh I live by faith in the Son of God, who loved me and gave Himself for me" (Galatians 2:20). In this remarkable verse the Apostle describes how he lived by faith in the Son of God. But he doesn't stop there; he adds "who loved me and gave Himself for me". As the Good Shepherd, Jesus spoke of giving His life for the sheep. The sacrificial love of Christ guides our life of faith in Him. We are guided by His love.

The Great Shepherd: God responded to the death of Christ in His resurrection. The resurrection of Christ demonstrates His power as the Great Shepherd of the sheep, who shed His blood and made one eternal sacrifice for sins, and now lives in the power of an endless life. We are guided by our living Shepherd, who had the power to lay down His life and to take it again (John 10:18), to fulfil God's will in our lives. The Father who could speak about His Son in whom He was well-pleased has the expectation of our lives being well-pleasing to Him. We are guided by His life.

The Chief Shepherd: A dear old friend of mine who managed a Christian bookshop was asked for a book called "The Blessed Hope" by Edward Dennett. He couldn't lay his hands on a copy and came into the office exclaiming, "I have lost the blessed hope!" The writers of the New Testament wrote to ensure that we never lose sight of the Blessed Hope. Paul reminds us to have this joyous event always in our sight: "Looking for the blessed hope and glorious appearing of our great God and Saviour Jesus Christ" (Titus 2:13). Peter also refers to the Morning Star in connection with the Lord's coming; a bright light leading us onwards and upwards (2 Peter 1:19). John calls it a purifying hope: "And everyone who has this hope in Him purifies himself, just as He is pure (1 John 3:3). We are guided by the light of His coming again.

Our Shepherd guides and shapes us by His love, His life and the light of His return.

Day 99

Sunday

Forsaken so we might never be forsaken

My God, My God, why have You forsaken Me?   (Psalm 22:1)

Psalms 22, 23 and 24 have often been referred to as the cross, the crook and the crown. They were written by King David, under the direction of the Holy Spirit, hundreds of years before the birth of Jesus Christ. These psalms refer prophetically to the coming Messiah and contemplate the past, present and future ministry of Christ. Psalm 22 looks back to His sufferings for us upon the cross and looks forward to the glorious results of those sufferings. In Psalm 23 we see His present shepherd-like care for us throughout our lives. And in Psalm 24 we look forward to the day when He will be owned as King of Kings and Lord of Lords.

The heart-rending opening verse of Psalm 22 leads us to an appreciation of what the Lord passed through at Calvary. It is important to see that the words are addressed to God. When we think of Calvary, we often concentrate upon the physical suffering the Lord endured at the hands of men. But the cross is about God's judgement against sin and His love for sinners. And the Lord Jesus had to pass through that judgement. As a Man here on earth, He had enjoyed complete communion with God. At the cross, He was forsaken by God. He was forsaken so that we might never be forsaken.

Psalm 22 can be divided into two sections: the sufferings of the cross (vv. 1-21a) and the glory of the cross (vv. 21b-31). There are seven statements which the Lord Jesus made from the cross. The fourth and central one was the opening words of Psalm 22: "My God, my God, why have You forsaken Me?" The Lord Jesus was the only man who ever had the right to ask God why He was forsaken. There was nothing in Him which deserved being abandoned by God at Calvary. But forsaken He was. It was God's judgement of sin and, as Paul reminds us in 2 Corinthians 5:21, God "made Him who knew no sin to be sin for us, that we might become the righteousness of God in Him." He bore God's judgement against sin so that we could escape it.

It is always difficult to write or speak about the sufferings of Christ. We tend to shy away from looking too deeply into what happened at the cross. It is holy ground, and we should approach the subject with a deep sense of reverence. The Lord Jesus instituted a means by which we would always remember His sacrifice for us. By nature, we can easily forget. Joseph asked the cupbearer, "When it is well with you, remember me." For a long time, the man forgot Joseph. I have to ask myself how easily I forget how much the Lord suffered for my salvation. Is it something in the distant past, or something I give thanks for every day of my life?

The Lord would always bring us around Himself. He never forgets us, and He never forsakes us. And it touches His heart when we by faith look up to Him in glory, remembering His love, responding in worship to His love and hastening in our hearts the day when He will return in love.

Day 100

Monday

Trust in the Lord

Trust in the LORD with all your heart,
And lean not on your own understanding;
In all your ways acknowledge Him,
And He shall direct your paths.

(Proverbs 3:5-6)

It is always good to pause at the beginning of a new working week to ensure we are trusting the Lord. Our responsibilities can be considerable, and we can dive into them, trusting our judgements and understanding without reference to the Lord. We can do things on autopilot and feel we only need to trust the Lord in the significant steps we take or when things go wrong. I know, when I retrace my actions, I often find my trust in the Lord was inconsistent.

The Lord always intended for us to trust Him with all our hearts all the time. There is not one aspect of our lives He is not interested in and in which He cannot make His presence known. Our enjoyment of fellowship with the Lord requires our complete trust. We see this clearly in the Old Testament. God was with Joseph in Potiphar's house and the prison. What Joseph learned from his adverse circumstances was that God was with him in his everyday life and prospered him. His experience equipped him to manage a great nation. Ruth learned to trust God on a farm and cheerfully undertook menial work to relieve the poverty she and Naomi were in. She became the great-grandmother of David. He worked every day as a shepherd, devoting himself to caring for his father's sheep. He learned the Lord was his shepherd, he learned courage, and he learned to worship. God chose him to be the King of Israel. Daniel learned to trust God to provide his necessary daily food; God prepared him for the highest office.

Paul writes in Colossians 3: "And whatever you do in word or deed, do all in the name of the Lord Jesus, giving thanks to God the Father through Him" (v. 17) and "Whatever you do, do it heartily, as to the Lord and not to men, knowing that from the Lord you will receive the reward of the inheritance; for you serve the Lord Christ" (vv. 23-24). Our trust in the Lord should be wholehearted and embrace every aspect of our lives. Even though we may have excellent skills, abilities and understanding, these are best used in humility and dependence upon the Lord. I have often discovered that the most capable people of God are the most gracious, lowly and self-effacing people.

If you go to Scone Palace in Scotland, you will find a mound with the following notice on it:

> Moot Hill or Boot Hill. Site of the coronations of the Kings of Scotland and of Scottish Parliaments. Artificial mound created by earth brought in the boots of lords swearing loyalty to their King

I saw this sign many years ago. It reminded me of how each of us is to bring all that we have and are to the Saviour. We are to trust Him every day of our lives and enjoy His fellowship. It is our privilege to rest in His wisdom and to always acknowledge His greatness from worshipping hearts. He will guide and bless us in the paths He has chosen for us.

Day 101

The great MD

But when He saw the multitudes, He was moved with compassion for them, because they were weary and scattered, like sheep having no shepherd. Then He said to His disciples, "The harvest truly is plentiful, but the labourers are few. Therefore pray the Lord of the harvest to send out labourers into His harvest."

(Matthew 9:36-38)

A brother had a hardware shop in the north of England, and salespeople would visit his shop to sell the latest products. One of these visitors would always ask the brother how his business was doing. He would say the company was doing well, because he had a great MD (Managing Director). After a few visits, the man said to the brother, "I always thought the business was yours; who is your MD?" The brother explained that he was a Christian, and he trusted the Lord for everything, including his business. This conversation was the start of many spiritual conversations with the salesperson. One day the man came to the brother's shop and explained that a friend of his was dying of cancer and asked if the brother would visit his sick friend. He readily agreed. When the brother arrived at the house, the man's wife explained that he was very poorly and so the visit would have to be short. The brother shared his faith with the dying man. Towards the end of the conversation, the man wanted to pray to the Lord for salvation. The brother described, in a simple way, how to pray to the Lord. At that moment the man's wife appeared. The brother knew he would have to leave: then the lady said, "I want to pray that prayer as well." And that afternoon the husband and his wife came to the Lord.

This all happened because a Christian made the opportunity to witness for the Lord in his everyday life. He didn't preach or give literature out; he simply brought the Lord into his conversation in a way which aroused the interest and attention of the people he met. The Lord did the same at Sychar's well when he said to the woman, "Give me a drink." From that simple request, the Lord began a conversation which led her in all her need to the Lord, and then she led others to Christ. A few verses later, Jesus said to His disciples, "I say to you, lift up your eyes and look at the fields, for they are already white for harvest!" (John 4:35).

We live in difficult times, and there is resistance to the Gospel. But the Lord lived in a spiritually bankrupt nation, riddled with hypocrisy and corruption, and occupied by foreign forces. Yet He said the fields were white to harvest. When He saw people in all their need, compassion filled His heart, and He wanted His disciples to respond in the same way. I have to ask myself, Am I in tune with the heart of the Lord when it comes to making opportunities to share His love? Sometimes we are fearful of people's reactions to our faith in Christ. Still, I have discovered over the years, especially with people at work, that those who can be the most antagonistic towards our faith in Christ are those who, in quieter moments, are prepared to listen.

Crisis creates concern. We are living in a worried world. An earthquake caused the Philippian jailer to ask the question "What must I do to be saved?" Perhaps the jailer's question is in more hearts than we realise. Let us ask the Lord to give us the grace and wisdom to know how to witness to the Saviour's love.

Day 102

Catching nothing

Children, have you any food?" They answered Him, "No."

(John 21:5)

It is extraordinary how the Lord uses the simplest of activities to teach us profound spiritual lessons. Peter had left his occupation as a fisherman to follow the Lord and become "a fisher of men" (Luke 5:1-11). In John 21 we see Peter returning to his occupation and taking others with him. That night they caught nothing. On the face of it, this seemed a pretty straightforward event. But it tells us so much about what happens when we decide to act in our own strength. Despite all our efforts and persistence, there is no blessing. Peter was not at peace, because he had denied the Lord, and the matter had not been settled. So what did he do? He went back to what he knew best. His friends and fellow disciples were equally unsettled and followed him. Peter, for all his failures, was a leader; wherever he went, others followed. How important it is to realise that, when we go in the wrong direction, we can also lead others to do the same.

But the incident also gives us an insight into how we should serve the Lord, particularly in evangelism. Fishing was a picture the Lord Jesus used in the Gospels to describe evangelising: "I will make you fishers of men." He visualises how the widespread preaching of the Gospel would lead vast multitudes to Himself. However, evangelism can never be successful unless it is done under the direction of the Lord and in the power of the Holy Spirit. Here, they had caught *nothing*, and the Lord told them in the most precise way, "Without Me you can do nothing" (John 15:5).

This wasn't the first time that Peter and his friends had toiled all night and caught nothing. In Luke 5, after speaking to the crowds, the Lord Jesus told Peter: "Launch out into the deep and let down your nets for a catch." Peter replied, "Master, we have toiled all night and caught nothing; nevertheless at Your word I will let down the net." That day they caught so many fish their nets began to break. But something else happened: Peter fell down at Jesus' knees, saying, "Depart from me, for I am a sinful man, O Lord!" He discovered that he was in the presence of the Person he would later confess as "the Christ, the Son of the living God" (Matthew 16:16). Peter was afraid, and felt a deep sense of his unworthiness. But the Lord said to him, "Do not be afraid. From now on, you will catch men." Then Peter and his friends forsook all and followed Jesus.

In the opening verses of John 21 we see the amazing grace of the Saviour. Whilst the disciples struggled, the Saviour waited for the moment when they realised all their efforts were fruitless and there was nothing more they could do. Then the Lord asked them a simple question, "Children, have you any food?" And they answered Him, "No." The Lord did not want them simply to discover weakness and fruitlessness, but to know Himself and His extraordinary grace. As we shall see, He is the source of all blessing.

Day 103

Thursday

It is the Lord!

Therefore that disciple whom Jesus loved said to Peter, "It is the Lord!"   (John 21:7)

After the disciples told the Lord they had caught nothing, He tells them to "cast the net on the right side of the boat", assuring them they would catch fish. And remarkably, they obey without question. This incident always reminds me of the simplicity of our service for the Lord. We are here to be His witnesses, and He is in heaven as our Lord and Saviour. He wants to guide us, both individually and in fellowship with one another into where and how He wants us to serve Him. The big difference between a fruitless night of fishing and a net full of fish was listening to and following the direction of the risen Saviour. The Lord had told them on more than one occasion where they would catch fish. He even told Peter to catch one fish (Matthew 17:27). So often we have an exercise to serve the Lord, and we put our heart and soul into the work, but sometimes we forget it is the Lord's work and we need His constant direction. David understood this when he wrote of God:

> I will instruct you and teach you in the way you
> should go;
> I will guide you with My eye (Psalm 32:8).

To be guided by someone's eye, we have to be looking into their faces. Paul also reminds us in 2 Corinthians 4:5-7: "For we do not preach ourselves, but Christ Jesus the Lord, and ourselves your bondservants for Jesus' sake. For it is the God who commanded light to shine out of darkness, who has shone in our hearts to *give* the light of the knowledge of the glory of God in the face of Jesus Christ." We are not preaching ourselves, but the Lord, and to do this, we must be guided by Him. We need to cultivate the habit of asking the Lord to direct our service precisely and then to follow Him in obedient and energetic faith.

When John witnessed the Lord's blessing, he said to Peter, "It is the Lord!" John is always associated with nearness to the Lord. He describes in four words the joy which was in his heart at the moment. He didn't keep this to himself; he shared it with his friend, Peter. We should never keep the impressions we have of the Saviour to ourselves, because by sharing them, we bring others close to the Lord. Peter was still burdened by his failure. But John's words did not cause him to say again, "Depart from me, for I am a sinful man, O Lord!" No, those words drew him to the Saviour, as he dragged the net to land in all the energy and purpose which would later mark him at Pentecost and in the house of Cornelius.

In John 1 we see the Lord in all His deity, and full of grace and truth. In the final chapter of his Gospel, we trace Christ's divinity in the guidance of simple fishermen who He was transforming into ministers of His grace and truth. To do this, he works in their hearts to teach them that He was the source of all power and blessing. As the lowly Nazarene He had manifested His grace and truth. And, in resurrection, He demonstrated the same beautiful features as He prepared a simple meal and invited His disciples into His presence: "Come and eat breakfast." John was later to write the Lord's words in Revelation 3:20: "If anyone hears My voice and opens the door, I will come in to him and dine with him, and he with Me." May we never cease to understand that it is in His presence we learn to serve Him better and He teaches us how to witness to His love and saving grace in this world.

Day 104

Friday

Dare to be a Dorcas

At Joppa there was a certain disciple named Tabitha, which is translated Dorcas. This woman was full of good works and charitable deeds which she did. (Acts 9:36)

Acts 9 begins with the conversion of Saul of Tarsus and leads on to a remarkable work of God in the extending of the Gospel and the growth of Christian assemblies. The chapter ends with the only mention of a woman called Tabitha. This was her Aramaic name, and we know her better as Dorcas, the Greek translation of her name, which means "gazelle". There is a small, beautiful gazelle called the dorcas gazelle (ariel gazelle). Its population is decreasing and it is classed as vulnerable in conservation terms.

Dorcas loved, and was loved. She teaches us about a ministry which has always characterised faithful Christian service. It is the ministry of doing good! We are told that her life was full of good works and charitable deeds. June often tells me, when I am driving, that her driving instructor said to her that every time we drive a car we should be kind to another motorist. She also reminds me she has been driving longer than me, so I should listen to her! Dorcas didn't just do a good deed for the day; she was full of good works and acts of love. For her, it was a way of life. She was following her Saviour. In the very next chapter, in the house of Cornelius, Peter speaks of how "God anointed Jesus of Nazareth with the Holy Spirit and with power, who went about doing good and healing all who were oppressed by the devil, for God was with Him" (Acts 10:38).

Dorcas had a particular and practical gift: she made clothes. When she died, the loss was felt so deeply that the brethren sent for Peter. When he met the widows who mourned her loss, they showed him the clothes she made. In the resurrection of Dorcas, Peter shows us how he had learned from his experience with the Lord Jesus in the house of Jairus (compare Mark 5). The Lord is always our model in service, whether we are making clothes or undertaking, as Peter was, extraordinary service for Him. The good works of Dorcas and her resurrection were both influential in leading people to the Lord (v. 42).

Dorcas had a heart for the Lord. She had a gift and the faith and determination to use it in His service. Dorcas didn't wait for an organisation or the support of others: she just got on with it. She served in love and followed the Saviour's example. Each of us has a gift from God, and we are not to neglect it: "Do not neglect the gift that is in you" (1 Timothy 4:14).

At the beginning of Acts 9, Saul of Tarsus, overwhelmed by the Lord's presence, said, "Lord, what do You want me to do?" (vv. 5-6, see also Acts 22:10). It was a question he would ask throughout his life as he sought the Lord's guidance. I think it was a question Dorcas asked and, most importantly, I think it is a question the Lord wants us to ask. The dorcas gazelle is a small, beautiful gazelle whose population is decreasing: we don't want this to happen amongst the people of God. Dare to be a Dorcas!

Day 105

Peacemakers

Therefore let us pursue the things which make for peace, and things by which one may edify another. (Romans 14:19)

It is God's desire that His people enjoy His peace and live in harmony with one with another. In Romans 14:19 Paul encourages us to "pursue the things which make for peace". It is an interesting verse because it suggests we encourage peace by doing things: by being busy. But the idea of pursuing is not chasing, but following. The Lord Jesus was always active in service, often to the point of exhaustion. When I get tired, I get irritable. But the Lord didn't. He was the "Prince of peace", and we learn to know and enjoy peace by following Him. The Lord's life seemed one of unrelenting pressure as He worked ceaselessly to demonstrate His love and grace in a needy world. He did this whilst being opposed, persecuted and rejected. But the Lord brought His peace into every circumstance.

I love to read Mark chapters 4 and 5. In these chapters, we see the Lord stilling the storm with the words, "Peace, be still!" (Mark 4:39). We love to see Legion at peace, "sitting and clothed and in his right mind" (Mark 5:15) and to hear Jesus say to the woman, "Daughter, your faith has made you well. Go in peace" (Mark 5:34). Then the Lord calmed Jairus' heart with the words, "Do not be afraid; only believe" (Mark 5:36) before filling his heart with joy when his daughter was restored to life. The Lord never avoided stormy circumstances: He brought His peace into those. circumstances.

We first knew "peace with God through our Lord Jesus Christ" (Romans 5:1), and we learned that "we have access by faith into this grace wherein we stand" (Romans 5:2). This enables us to live in peace before Him. Prayer is the means by which we practically experience "the peace of God, which surpasses all understanding". This is the peace which guards our hearts and minds through Christ Jesus (Philippians 4:7). As we enjoy peace through faith and prayer, we will seek those things which promote peace in our families, our fellowship and amongst our fellow human beings.

We do this by being spiritually minded, not earthly-minded. Cares and riches create worry but "to be spiritually minded is life and peace" (Romans 8:6). Peace is one of the beautiful characteristics of the fruit of the Spirit, and He enables us to enjoy and transmit this peace in our lives: "But the fruit of the Spirit is love, joy, peace" (Galatians 5:22). We also need to act in the wisdom that is from above: "But the wisdom that is from above is first pure, then peaceable, gentle, willing to yield, full of mercy and good fruits, without partiality and without hypocrisy. Now the fruit of righteousness is sown in peace by those that make peace" (James 3:17-18). It is by being gracious with one another that we fulfil our responsibility to endeavour "to keep the unity of the Spirit in the bond of peace" (Ephesians 4:3). And we should always seek to be peacemakers:

> "Blessed are the peacemakers,
> For they shall be called sons of God" (Matthew 5:9).

May God's peace fill our hearts to calm our days and powerfully witness to our Saviour.

About the Author

Gordon Kell has been involved in Christian ministry for over fifty years. Apart from a period of five years in full-time Christian service, this has always been in a "tentmaking" capacity. With his wife, June, their Christian ministry has included young peoples' work, camps, Christian holidays, young married couples' weekends, and conferences throughout the UK and occasionally in Europe. Until recently, Gordon's written ministry was linked with his long involvement in radio Bible teaching. Gordon and June have one daughter, three granddaughters and a grandson, and live in Northern Lincolnshire, not far from the birthplace of John Wesley who once said, "Let your words be the genuine picture of your heart."

Gordon commands a wide respect for "rightly handling the word of truth" (2 Timothy 2:15), combining awareness of its depth with succinctness and a personable style.

Lightning Source UK Ltd.
Milton Keynes UK
UKHW050644230622
404802UK00015B/1930

9 780951 151587